Sharing her story, Adrienne makes you feel like you have walked with her on a spiritual journey. Her love of God, her husband, family, friends and the beauty of nature shines throughout. She has shown us that although life gives us many challenges, new doors keep opening and the light shines through.

—Valarie Collins

Adrienne writes about her amazing life experiences in a light, engaging manner, speaking with refreshing openness about the good, the bad, and the ugly, while maintaining a positive and resilient attitude. In a day and age when everyone pretends that their lives are perfect, Adrienne openly reveals her doubts and scars, as well as her triumphs and joys. For anyone who has dealt with adversity, this is a highly relatable and uplifting read.

—Cheryl Janish

This One Time is a story of redemption and healing. It reminds us that life is often unfair, but God is good and He has the last move! It is a journey of courage, as Adrienne just keeps taking the next step forward. Bravo!

—Zeta MacDonald

This is a story of faith and resiliency, of knowing God in good times and in hard times. Reading *This One Time*, I felt that I was sitting down and listening to a friend share her life story. At times mesmerizing, at other times poignant, and always honest, Adrienne's unique memoir will help all of us ask how God has been with us and what we have learned on the journey of life. Highly recommended.

—Diane Roth

March 2022

This One Time...

Adrienne Poppe

This One Time...

One Woman's Personal Journey

through loss and darkness to find faith,
community, purpose and love

By Adrienne Melanie Poppe

Green
Fire
Press

Housatonic
Massachusetts

Cover photo: a quilt made by the author, Adrienne Melanie Poppe (technique and design inspired by Ann Loveless).

Cover and page design by Anna Myers Sabatini

Cataloging-in-Publication data

Name: Poppe, Adrienne Melanie, author.

Title: This one time: one woman's personal journey through loss and darkness to find faith, community, purpose and love / by Adrienne Melanie Poppe.

Description: Housatonic, MA: Green Fire Press, 2021.

Identifiers: LCCN: 2021917456
ISBN: 978-1-7347571-2-5 (paperback) | 978-1-7347571-3-2 (ebook)

Subjects: LCSH | Poppe, Adrienne Melanie. | Women—Biography. | Cults—Biography. | Disabled women—Biography. | Christian biography. | Spiritual biography. | BISAC BIOGRAPHY & AUTOBIOGRAPHY / Personal Memoirs | BIOGRAPHY & AUTOBIOGRAPHY / Women | BIOGRAPHY & AUTOBIOGRAPHY / Religious | BIOGRAPHY & AUTOBIOGRAPHY / People with Disabilities

Classification: LCC BL72 .P67 2021 | DDC 291.4/092—dc23

Green
Fire
Press

Green Fire Press
PO Box 377 Housatonic MA 01236

Contents

PART THREE

To my parents, who taught me by example how to navigate life's difficulties with grace and how to keep alive the idea of endless possibilities.

And to my beloved husband Oscar, who loved me before I loved myself; you are my compass and my hero.

Prologue

In 1997 I was RV camping in Chattanooga, Tennessee with my husband Oscar and our two grandchildren, Eddie and Aubrey. Eddie was 6 and his cousin Aubrey was 7.

Over dinner one night we began sharing. Eddie started. With his elbow resting on the table and his hand in the air he began, "You know...this one time...." And on he went with his story. We all watched and listened intently, urging him on with "ah huh," "yeah," which encouraged him to elaborate in detail, obviously so delighted to have our undivided attention.

Before he could finish taking his last breath, Aubrey began, "Well...this one time...." and off she was telling us *her* story. We were all delighted. They were happy in the telling, and we were delighted in the listening. We were serious and giggling and just enjoying each other's company so very much.

During the rest of the trip, they were continually sharing stories of times in their young lives. Each time, without thinking, they would break the silence with "This one time...." We would all laugh and ask "Yes?"

It's become a family code phrase for "I want to share a story, everyone please listen." We smile and we listen.

Over the years when I have told a story from my life, to an old friend or new one, so many times the response is the same: "You really should write a book!" I've always known I had some interesting and unusual stories, but it was that week with Eddie and Aubrey that inspired me. I knew then that all I had to do was simply start sharing and begin with "This one time...."

Introduction

Strategies of Resilience

This is the story of my determination and resilience. In reflecting on my life, it helps to look back with compassion, learn from my mistakes, rejoice in my victories and continue to grow. I believe that every day I have choices regarding who I want to be and where I want to go. Being aware is half the battle. I have travelled through great darkness and found my way to the light. I have developed strategies to overcome challenges and live a productive and creative life. I gathered the necessary tools: dreaming and goal setting, staying connected with community and family, cultivating my faith and exploring and developing creative passions. I hope that my stories and strategies will enrich your journey and encourage you to entertain the notion of keeping your heart and mind open.

Planning is a big part of my life. I feel better when there is a plan. In the quiet wee hours of the morning, with a cup of coffee, I study the calendar, not wanting to miss a family event and taking care to organize the business of life. It clears my mind of the clutter and noise of the world so that I can reward myself with time to do the things that bring me peace, comfort and purpose.

I love to dream. There is an art to creating a dream and breaking it down into small steps so that I can try to make it reality. I'm a goal setter too, but it is the creative journey and making bold choices that gives me energy and clarity.

This one time...on a hike in Big Bend National Park, half way up the mountain, I was so weak and tired. Folks coming down the path saw me struggling and they offered sweet encouragement by telling me there was a place to rest up ahead, just around the next bend. "Go on, you can make it." It was touching and I was so appreciative of their encouragement. Now, tears fill my heart as I recognize how blessed I am to have had people helping me along every path of my life, believing in me and encouraging me. I want to pass that on. It defines why community is so important to me. We support and serve each other, cheering each other on and lending an ear when someone needs to be heard.

The American author and illustrator Sark said, "There are circles of women around us that weave invisible nets to carry us when we are weak and sing with us when we are strong." I find strength with my dear circle of friends who know me well enough to sense when to throw out the nets and when to simply grab my hand and sing and dance. Being able to be vulnerable and open about my thoughts and feelings and weaknesses makes room for intimacy and love. It is my sincere hope that when you hear my vulnerability in these pages, you are touched with the desire to be vulnerable, open and honest in your own life.

By the age of 30, I had already lived a life filled with obstacles. Then I met Oscar, the love of my life. We have shared dreams, desires and magical moments, as well as difficulties, grief and failure. It was our destiny to be together and we are persistent in our commitment to each other's happiness. We share a passion that is rare and valuable, always wanting the best for each other. Like a rainstorm that produces a rainbow, our lives have been filled with many storms, but then beautiful rainbows appear, keeping us always looking up.

Pursuing a passion that promotes creativity is very important to me. As parents, we encourage our youth to explore and learn activities such as music, drama, art, 4-H club and team sports. Many different and varied passions fill my life, mostly revolving around artistic expression, like gardening, cooking, entertaining or needlework. Travel is another very strong passion that calls to my soul. Enticed to a faraway place or perhaps an event like a balloon festival or a music festival, the planning begins. In this book I will be sharing some of my travel adventures. They are significant partly because the dream of travel was the common thread of passion that initially brought my true love and I together and has held us close through the last thirty-seven years. Travel also holds a certain spiritual element for me because it allows me to see the world through another lens. It speaks to my soul, connecting and grounding me so that I remember that the world is bigger than just me, me, me.

Up until the year 2000 I had a brown thumb. Then I realized I wanted to learn about growing things. Now, I love to dig in the dirt. I love to see the buds in the spring. I love to water the plants in the dry hot summer and see them breathe again when autumn is in the air. It is a peaceful passion that did not come naturally to me, but when I declared I wanted to learn, I began with a dream and brought it to life. The garden also helps me understand the patience required in life to get through the winter of my soul and to appreciate and see the joyous growth in the spring.

I also love to open my home to friends and family, showering them with good food and a comfortable place to share and enjoy each other's company. After all, entertaining is a form of art. It takes practice and skill to gracefully set the stage. Recipes and cooking are creative and artistic and so is setting the tables and picking out the music that will play in the background. The best part of entertaining is encouraging others to tell their stories. It is satisfying to witness my friends and family as their bodies fill with energy from sharing. Then, sometimes they let out a big breath and sigh as they share a burden they've been carrying. They so appreciate being seen and heard. It's good for them to share with laughter and tears, and seeing them helps me as I listen and learn with empathy and admiration.

It's important to socialize and stay engaged as we age. I love a friendly, casual game of bridge. It's challenging and civilized. The strategy is intricate. The bidding is like being a code talker or learning a foreign language. The playing calls for keen memory.

Dancing is also important to me. I love the exercise and energy. We can be anywhere and dance. My husband and I often break into dance in the living room. It adds a little spring to our step to share a lively tune, kicking up our heels, or a tender and touching quiet embrace as we sway to a soft melody.

One of my greatest passions was ignited around the year 2009, when I stepped into the world of quilting. It started with a simple idea—warm coverings needed for world relief. A remnant and a thread ignited a marvelous passion that helps me create beautiful works of art and brings me great joy and peace. I love the challenge of learning something new and the satisfaction of finishing a quilt. I also enjoy the friendships that are fostered as I reach out to the community that shares my same passion.

An Amish quilt is designed to include a mistake in each quilt, because nothing manmade is perfect and yet it is still beautiful. I find grace and comfort knowing that although I am imperfect, still I can be beautiful. It's OK to make a mistake. I have to be able to forgive myself for mistakes and get back up and try again. That is an internal strength that I believe can be developed and learned. We say practice makes perfect as we teach our children to read or play a sport or a musical instrument. Well—the same can be said for learning coping skills for life. I hope hearing about my passions will inspire you to find yours.

I was born a Jewish girl, converted to Christianity as a teen-ager and then spent seven years in a religious cult. The up side of those years was that I found faith and life-long friends. The down side was some of the controlling messages of shame recorded on reels that still run over and over in my mind. Some of my beliefs don't fall into a specific denomination or faith. God and I have worked it out. I have a personal relationship with God, which is quite amazing in and of itself, but perhaps even more because of my unique faith journey.

I choose, in this writing, to be open and share myself with the hope that you see how liberating it can be. In these pages, you will see that I am many things. I am vulnerable. I am also strong. I am determined, trustworthy and dependable. I am a survivor. I can be melancholy. I am curious. I am an artist. Perhaps if I am willing to be vulnerable, also sharing the darkness that I sometimes walk in, it will help others to know they are not alone.

The COVID pandemic has changed everything. In addition to the hundreds of thousands of lives lost, families and friends have been split apart by anger and fear. Isolation fueled the depression that haunts many. I pray as our world emerges from the COVID shutdown that we heal relationships and find positive strategies to fight the growing mental health issues that exist.

Thank you for sharing this journey with me. I hope you are touched and inspired by the story of my personal evolution—how I followed my dreams and overcame challenges, building the joyous and fulfilling life I live now. The facts may have blurred some with time, but my memories are true to me; this is how they are stored in my soul.

My daughter asked me about a decade ago to write the story of her maternal grandfather. He died before she was born and so she didn't know him. To honor my daughter's request, my story begins with my dad, Leonard.

PART ONE

Leonard

This one time...in Chicago, Illinois, around 1940, two brothers went out for the night. Mel had a date, and they were on the prowl looking for a date for Leonard. As they drove and chatted, Leonard realized that he really wanted to be on the date with his brother Mel's girl. He devised a plan, and by the end of the night he figured out a way to ask Luella out for himself. Leonard was tall and handsome, with thick wavy brown hair and kind hazel eyes, perfectly spaced on his face. He looked like a movie star. Luella was a petite beauty with well-defined features and she was well educated, though from a poor family. She lived in a room behind the upholstery store with her parents, her brother Aaron and her sister Adriana, who had Downs Syndrome. They talked about the future and Leonard told her about his job and the money he had in the bank. She was impressed with his nice car too. On the third date, Leonard asked Luella to marry him... and she said yes. A short 10 days later, they were married. Not long after, Luella would find out that the car wasn't paid for, there was no money in the bank, and there was no job.

Then World War II happened and Leonard went to war, joining the Army Air Corps as a pilot, flying B-24 Liberators. Not long after he left for war, their first child was born. Sharon was about a year and a half old when he came home, ready to reacquaint himself with Luella, get to know his daughter and begin building a life. The prospects were out there—the new American dream. Leonard's dream was always just around the corner, down the road or in another city. He always saw the possibilities...endless possibilities. He was filled with great ideas, and the desire to build his dream. After Chicago, there was Indianapolis and then Louisville... and a son produced in each city.

My parents, Leonard and Luella

In 1952 prosperity was on the rise. Telephones and televisions were finding their way into most homes. Jobs were plentiful. Despite the Korean War, Americans were ready to succeed. Leonard had some brilliant ideas working in his mind. He kept his ear to the ground, listening for opportunities. He was anxious to leave the dreary, cold, dark cities back East that he had known. California, the land of sunshine and opportunity, called to forward-thinking, creative minds filled with hope for a bright future.

Leonard knew all Californians wanted swimming pools, but not every average family could have their own pool. He dreamed of a section of tract homes sharing one common pool. A small monthly fee would take care of the cost. It would have been the first association of its kind. What about a store front building with washing machines and dryers? People would pay to use his community machines. It would have been one of the first laundromats in southern California. *Thank you, Dad, because I know my ability to dream came from you.*

The dreams called and so did his friend, Ralph Sampson. Load 'em up and head 'em out. We're going to California!

There was a job with Sears selling appliances. He could always sell things. There were water purifiers, draperies, carpeting, and musical organs. He was also great as a short order cook and so at some point he got himself a restaurant in Glendale and called it the Buggy Whip. He loved owning his own business. Luella was not thrilled with the restaurant and the long, hard hours they both had to put in to keep the doors open. It wasn't too long before Leonard was back in sales, relying on commissions to keep food on the table. Maybe some of those special Sunday night dinners of silver dollar pancakes weren't the dream projected but, in fact, the reflection of no sales, no money and no food. But Leonard was not defeated. He was always looking just around the corner, like a miner panning for gold.

Luella was always looking too—at houses. That was their Sunday entertainment. The model homes were so beautifully decorated and the landscaping meticulous. More dreams—maybe more possibilities. Why not—it's America! The beautiful model homes inspired Leonard and Luella, filling them with ideas. He'd walk the length of something like a window valance, pacing it off or getting up close to examine it underneath. He'd draw what he was seeing in the air, with his hands. He was extraordinarily handy and talented. He could just look at something and know how to recreate it. He could tear down walls, recreate valances, make gold leaf desks and mosaic tables, rewire things, design and create amazing landscape designs, including tiki huts, in-ground barbeque pits and meticulous putting greens.

Leonard and Luella were talented, creative and smart. They would often find a new place for us to live—not a model home, just a different place. Some years later I asked my mother about all the houses, so many houses. She said, when dreams were coming true, they'd move up, securing a nicer place for us to live. But when times were lean, they would find someone who wanted to trade houses. They would give those folks our nicer house in even exchange for a smaller, not so nice, house that was less expensive and easier to manage. They didn't mind because it gave them more projects to do, using all their creative ideas.

Leonard may have tricked Luella into marriage, but if it was trickery, it was done with good intentions. Love at first sight might do that to you. They were good parents. Seldom did Leonard raise his voice and neither did Luella. They were not demonstrative with each other nor with us; there wasn't much affection and kissing, though I do remember hugs and a little silliness. Maybe it was the accepted parent-child distance of the "Leave it to Beaver" culture of the time. They were not terribly successful, but Dad earned an adequate wage, always keeping food on the table and a roof over our heads. He might have done better if he had continued as a travelling salesman, but this one time...someone tried to break into the house when Dad was gone. They bought a dog and Leonard quit travelling. His career after that was not terribly successful but he was home at night. They took life in stride and taught by example to roll with the punches. Leonard continued his pursuit of the dream and the endless possibilities.

Mom and Dad, thank you for teaching me to live within my means. Thank you for teaching me to give a good day's work for a good day's pay and to be grateful for the work. Thank you for teaching me to stretch a nickel to a dime. Thank you for being creative. I love knowing these things that live on in me I inherited from you.

Polio

Luella had three beautiful children, a daughter and two sons. Then she had two miscarriages, which left her wanting another child. She hoped for another daughter. In 1954, just two years after their move to California, Luella gave birth to her fourth child, a girl. I was named Adrienne Melanie Sholdar.

I am three years old. The night is black. It's raining outside. I'm in bed hoping to fall asleep. I'm alone in the bedroom because my sister is out with her friends. I'm so scared. I keep hearing noises outside my bedroom window.

"Mom... Mom...." I cry out. No answer. There's a crash against the window. Someone must be out there.

"Mom!" I call louder. I can't get up. I'm paralyzed with polio. I'm paralyzed with fear. "If you don't settle down young lady, I'm going to come in there with a hair brush," she warned.

"Please check, Mom. I'm so scared."

I'm so tired. I want to go to sleep. Then, I remember the plants under my window. They are beating on the glass. *I'm safe.*

In 1956, a bad batch of the polio vaccine was distributed back East. People didn't know what to do, including my folks. They decided to wait to have our family vaccinated until the news reported that the vaccines were OK.

There was a picnic at a nearby park with lots of families. What harm could there be in a weekend picnic? We went. A short time later my legs began to hurt. Every time my dad would touch my legs, I'd cry out in pain. My mom just knew it was polio. My God, the fear that surely gripped them. Fear for me, their 2-year-old toddler, and fear for the older siblings in the house, my 13-year-old sister and my brothers, ages 7 and 10. They feared for the neighbors exposed. My dad, Leonard, was only 34 years old. He didn't make a lot of money. He was a jack of all trades and a master of none, working hard to keep us in a lower middle-class lifestyle. They had four children to feed and now their toddler was paralyzed. What would the future hold?

"She'll never walk again," said the first doctor. It was spinal paralytic polio.

"She'll never walk again," said ten more doctors.

We went from doctor to doctor.

"There is nothing we can do," they said.

"I don't believe it. I won't believe it," my mother declared.

The twelfth doctor said, "Maybe there is something we can do." My mother, Luella, was a determined woman. *Thank you for your persistence, Mom.*

Imagine what was going through my parents' minds. In the early 1950's the threat of polio was coming to an end. It was not an epidemic anymore. How could this be? Six weeks of quarantine was imposed immediately. They took me away from my family to be quarantined at Kaiser Permanente. I was too young to remember what the place was like, but the separation was traumatic—for me, for my parents and well, for the whole family. They were scared for me of course, but they were also scared for those I may have unknowingly infected with the crippling virus. Six weeks was a long, long time for everyone.

My legs hurt and I would cry in pain if anyone touched them. I was so scared. I couldn't move my legs. I couldn't move one arm and I couldn't sit up on my own. There were braces made for my legs and feet that were shoes with a bar in between that could be adjusted. The polio had turned my legs and feet inward and the doctors were hoping to straighten them and pull them back into place. My feet were crippled and beginning to become deformed.

I remember this one time...I was dragging myself by one arm, the other arm and my dead legs dragging behind with those awkward heavy braces, down the hallway from my bedroom to the living room. I was three years old.

My folks went into huge debt to build a swimming pool in the backyard so they could put me through the recommended Sister Kenny water exercises. Every day there was water therapy and Dad would also massage my legs and push on the balls of my feet, stretching the muscles, willing them to work again.

Polio is a highly infectious disease caused by a virus that invades the nervous system. As the virus grows it destroys nerve cells (motor neurons), which talk to muscles. The muscles have no instructions so they don't work. The destruction spread through my nervous system and I regressed. In addition to being paralyzed in both legs and one arm, I was back in diapers and using a baby bottle too.

It took two years of intense physical therapy. Then suddenly I recovered. For any toddler, the first two years is a progression of learning to walk, talk, give up the bottle and master potty training. For me, at age two, polio hit the reset button so that I needed to learn it all over again. By age four I was walking again. I held on to the bottle for a little while longer.

I remember one day standing in the garage looking out the door to the street with the nipple of the baby bottle just hanging between my teeth. I'm shaking the bottle back and forth, up and down, and back and forth again. *How far can I shake it before it hits me in the face? When will they get home and see me? I'm standing! Look at me! I'm standing.*

My siblings: Sharon at the top, Terry on left,
me in the middle and Mickey on the right, around 1958

The Hollywood Years

This one time...on a day in 1959, my dad, Leonard, was working with a man who was a part-time Hollywood agent. My brother Mickey went to work with Dad and was "discovered." Someone saw something in him and said he should try to be in television. Mickey was 10, which made me 5 years old. The next decade would become, to me, "The Hollywood Years."

Our family was middle class and we continued to live that way. The only exception was that my brother was a movie star. He started with small parts for the first several years. Then in 1962 he landed a role in a series, "The Farmer's Daughter," starring William Windom and Inger Stevens. Mickey would go to a set every day for filming, and since he was only 13 years old, our mother went with him. He would rehearse his lines over and over, always prepared. In the next decade he would work with some very famous people, including Bob Hope and Lucille Ball in "The Facts of Life" and James Garner and Kim Novak in "Boys Night Out." It was big time.

Mickey was always just Mickey to me, but my life was very different now. My older sister was already married and living in another city. My other brother was away at college, and Mickey and my mother were away at the set every day. I'd come home each day from school to a very quiet house with only a maid there. She would iron and cook and be there to make sure I wasn't alone, but there was no conversation or nurturing. They were quiet years for me, and more than a little bit lonely.

About the time Mickey started the series my parents thought maybe I'd like to try and get acting parts too. They took me to a photographer for a photo shoot so I'd have what I needed to audition. My mom or dad took me on several auditions, but I was too shy to get noticed. Then, when I was 8 years old, there was an episode on my brother's series that they wanted me to play in. I was so excited to think of being on a television show. Mom said, "You can do it." I looked at my professional photos and thought I was cute. I was so scared, but I didn't tell anyone. I wished I could blend into the walls and disappear. The episode was about a birthday party for one of the young characters on the show. I was to be one of the kids at the party.

"I can do this," I tell myself. But what if someone speaks to me? What do I say? My stomach is so sick. How did I get the part? I didn't go on an interview or attend a cattle call. They must have seen my picture and think I'm cute but, oh...I hope no one talks to me. There is so much noise. The lights are bright. Everyone is talking as they set up the stage. I don't see Mickey. He's probably in his trailer doing his school work. I thought he'd be right here, but the scene is with Rory, his little brother on the show. Lights—action—lots of action and buzz. Then the background is quiet and the cameras move into the set. The director shouts, "Lights, action!" Children are running around the couch on the living room set, squealing loudly because it's a birthday party. "Cut!" It's over. It's a wrap. I am so uncomfortable and nervous. What happened? It's already over. *"I don't ever want to do this again," I think. "Mom will be disappointed."*

I'm not sure if she really was disappointed. I know she thought I was adorable and they knew how to get me in the door to follow in Mickey's footsteps. It was disappointing to not even try, but I was so darn shy. I was afraid of my own shadow. Perhaps if I had been willing, I would have had more time with my parents during the ten years Mickey was acting. Mom stayed very involved with Mickey and spent less time with me.

Since I didn't take to acting, there was a brief time when I was around 14 when my mother thought that perhaps modeling would be right for me. Looking at my very petite body, she said,

"They won't want you for runway work, but perhaps you can do camera work or hand modeling." She thought I had beautiful hands because her hands were a petite size 5, but my hands were a large size 8. She enrolled me in modeling school. As part of the classes, I learned to walk a runway. *Hold your stomach in—core tight, stand straight. Heel...toe. Place heel just in front of toe on the other foot at 6 o'clock. Keep the neck long. Head straight and chin down ever so slightly so you can balance a book on your head. Now walk to the end, pause, turn gracefully, continue.*

I don't remember graduating from modeling school or pursuing anything related to modeling. I do remember bathing suit photo shoots. I had on a bikini and wore a hair piece and the make-up of the day, which was white eye shadow and dark black "twiggy" eyelashes, which were painted on little black lines mimicking eyelashes. These days mascara bothers me so much that I only wear it for fancy events.

I think my mother wanted me to be a model. She thought I was pretty, but painfully shy and that this would perhaps help me come out of my shell. She had contacts and gumption, but my dad didn't like the idea, I don't know why. It wasn't very important to me so I didn't try to pursue it. Looking back, I'm not sure if my mother had modeling in mind or was just helping me to learn to disguise my disability. She never came out and said this and I don't think she meant it in a bad way. Perhaps she just knew my choices in life would be greater if people didn't know I had a disability. After all, it was the 1960's, and alongside the civil rights movement advocates were beginning to speak out on rights for people with disabilities. A disability would be a third strike against me, since I was already female and Jewish. I think Mom just wanted me to blend in, and since I was so shy that suited me fine. I do believe that experience helped to build my confidence. Better posture helped in job interviews throughout my life and in the social settings my later life would include.

The Cancer Ward

It was quiet as we sat in the living room, all feeling very blue. My sister and brothers had all come home to the apartment where mom and I were currently living in Reseda, California. Dad was mostly living at the hospital because of his cancer. It was Christmas time and since the hospital denied his request for a day pass to come home, this would be our first Christmas without our dad. The silver tree was up and the presents were wrapped sitting underneath the tree just waiting for him. Now what should we do? Should we carry them all to the hospital? Or would that just make him feel worse?

There we sat in sunny southern California, needing sunshine in our lives. Someone said, "Let's open the presents and have Christmas right now." It was perfect. We laughed and enjoyed the giving and love shared by thoughtful gifts. Piles of wrapping paper filled the living room floor and we all had our gifts stacked in front of us. Everyone seemed determined to put on a happy face. Perhaps some of it was for me, because I was the youngest. Perhaps it was for my mother, who faced the hardest journey. We enjoyed this little boost and then resumed our intimate quietness.

A short while later the phone rang. When you have a loved one in the hospital, the ring of a telephone comes with anxiety. I don't remember who answered the phone, but when they hung up, they had big news. "They've granted dad's day pass. He's coming home for Christmas!"

Oh my gosh. We all knew exactly what we had to do. We rewrapped all the presents and placed them back underneath the tree. The next day when dad came home, we shared Christmas all over again, opening the presents and pretending to be surprised. The surprise was pretend, but the joy of being together was real. *It was one of the best Christmases of my life.*

In 1968, when I was 14 and Dad was 48 years old, he was told he had ear, nose and throat cancer and had only six months to live. Two years later, he was still fighting the fight. He endured a great deal and lost a great deal. His body failed him. He had one of the large muscles running down the side of his neck removed. Then they removed the other one, along with the roof of his mouth.

He is so quiet. Does his voice hurt? I don't ask. We just sit quietly. Every day Mom picks me up from school and we drive to the Miami Veterans' Hospital to the cancer ward to sit. There are eight beds in Dad's room—all men, all veterans, all dying. It's so hard not to look at them—not to smell them. The smell of death and cancer is strong. The sound of it is silence. The cancer has eaten a hole the size of a quarter straight through the side of my dad's cheek. I count the tiles in the room over and over. The man in the corner is smoking, puffing a cigarette through the tracheotomy in his throat.

If I focus, I can still hear the noise and clatter of hospital carts and folks chatting, bells ringing and meals being shared, but in this ward, everybody is waiting—waiting for death. My dad was a Pall Mall man. He started smoking during World War II and he smoked for more than twenty years before his ear, nose and throat cancer diagnosis. My mother was a smoker as well, as were my sister and both brothers. In fact, I recall standing in a hospital hall listening to a doctor's diagnosis and the minute the doctor stopped talking the entire family lit up a cigarette. I was too young. Yes, back then you could smoke in a hospital. I have a vague recollection of my parents suggesting the cancer was caused by some chemical exposure my dad may have experienced during World War II, but surely, we can't dismiss the risk he took by heavily smoking for twenty years.

I thought for sure I'd never smoke, and I stuck to that decision until I was 24 years old, after which I smoked more than a pack a day for twenty years. One of the hardest things I ever did was quit nicotine, but it was the best thing I ever did. As of this writing I have been nicotine-free for more than twenty-five years. Medical reports indicate that seven years after quitting smoking, your lungs rejuvenate, as if you had never smoked. I still regret the years I smoked when my children were small and the bad influence that was for them.

As the months clicked by beyond his six-month death sentence, my dad's dreams resurfaced. We moved to Florida because he realized he wanted to spend his last days with his brothers, who lived there. Dad went there to scout it out while Mom and I stayed in California. He found a senior condominium community and fell in love with it, writing to assure me it would be a wonderful life and we would be happy. There was a lake for fishing and a swimming pool. Once there, my parents made lots of friends quickly. They played bridge and dad got a little fishing boat. We shared nice family gatherings with his brothers and their small families. He enjoyed the reconnection with his brothers and a taste of retirement. He knew he didn't have long. He hoped to have us settled in a secure life before his final departure, but my mother missed her three older children who had stayed in California and the life we knew there.

There were no other children in the complex. I was still shy and made no friends at my new school. Those were more quiet and lonely years for me. Dad was peaceful. He'd fish during the day. Sometimes he and I would go to the billiard room and shoot pool. The best times were when my folks had friends in to play bridge. I loved sitting so close to my dad and feeling part of him and the game. I could hear and feel him breathing. He'd point to which card I should play from his hand. Dad was an excellent bridge player. You could hear a pin drop in the room while everyone quietly concentrated on their playing.

Time marched on. After his diagnosis in 1968, we moved to Florida, then back to California, only to find ourselves back in

Florida in 1970. I was numb after so many years in the cancer ward—day in, day out—waiting—another surgery—another hope—another day of "the ward." I felt nothing, because if I dared to feel something, I was afraid the flood of guilt and tears would drown me. I felt guilty for my desire to be somewhere else while my dad was dying and my mother was so very tired. *They need me.* Tears of exhaustion simmer. *We cannot give up.* Life moves on all around us. Dad was "silent movie star" strong. He was our rock, worrying about us, not himself. Another six months passed and eating became difficult for him. Mom would gently insert a long tube through his nose. She would blend all the food, hold the end of the tube high above Dad's head and pour the blended food through a funnel. The food moved ever so slowly down the tube. It was an intimate and deeply personal process. Dad would spend the last year of his life between the Miami VA cancer ward and a high-rise condominium on Biscayne Boulevard in North Miami, Florida.

The gentleness my mother showed in her caregiving for Dad would be one of the biggest lessons I would learn from her. My dad's graceful acceptance, always carrying himself with dignity, is the part of him I remember the most. Even when he wore a scarf covering the lower half of his face so others would not have to see the devastation the cancer had wrought, his gentle hazel eyes still showed me tenderness.

Conversion

Unrest and discontent filled the minds and streets of America in the 1960's. The war in Vietnam was escalating, and in 1964 US ships were fired upon in an incident known as the Gulf of Tonkin. The United States stepped up its involvement. In 1965, looting, violence and chaos took over the streets of the Watts area of South Central Los Angeles. Raging fires, tempers and fears went on for 6 long days. The Beatles broke up.

By 1969, protests against Vietnam broke out on college campuses across the United States. We were shocked as we watched the reports that student demonstrators were shot on the campus of Kent State University.

While all this anger raged, quietly the streets filled with the chants and dancing of the Hare Krishna. Draped in robes, they shaved their heads and surrendered their lives, money, intelligence and words, in exchange for a life centered on their God.

A new generation known as hippies searched for spiritual consciousness through drugs. In 1970 the people of America were very angry. Ten years of Vietnam tore at them. There was a great feeling of unrest in the country.

That year, my high school decided to try a new class schedule system called modules that ran similar to a college schedule. I'd have history for perhaps three mods consecutively, twice per week in a lecture hall. A mod was twenty minutes. While typing was two mods, five days a week, most classes were only 2 or 3 days a week. There were students constantly roaming campus, milling around, killing time between classes. It was chaos. Nobody knew who should or shouldn't be in class, and so there was a constant flow of kids coming and going everywhere. We were even allowed to leave campus. Sometimes I'd walk to the grocery store and get some fruit for lunch. Occasionally I'd walk to the local hangout, a fried chicken place, for one chicken wing. Dollars were tight. Dad was on Social Security disability living at the VA hospital and Mom could only work part-time, allowing for time to visit with Dad.

Mostly, I'd find an out-of-the-way spot in a grassy courtyard and try to disappear. I was overwhelmed by the chaos. There was chaos in the country, chaos on the campus and chaos in my soul.

I was always the outsider. Seven schools in ten years had made me shy and detached. Now I spent every afternoon and every weekend at the VA hospital in a cancer ward with my dad and seven other men with the worst cancers imaginable, all near the end of their lives. My soul was sad and searching.

My family was Jewish. My older siblings all went to Hebrew school. Mom kept me home on Yom Kipper and Rosh Hashanah, the Jewish high holidays, out of respect for our religion. While we did celebrate Hanukkah occasionally, I never went to temple and never had a discussion with my parents about God or faith. But every day I saw death knocking at the door of the men I spent my time with and it left me searching.

A few years earlier, a boy at school had given me a charm. When my mother found the Saint Christopher medal in my dresser drawer, she was very upset. I didn't even know what it was, other than a gift from a boy—a sign that someone liked me! I knew my older brother had studied world religion and he was brilliant and a hero to me, so I picked up some religious books and started to read about various religions, always hiding the books.

One day, as I sat on the grass in the corner of the courtyard at school, Chuck came over to me, sat down and said, "hi there." I don't remember how I knew Chuck, but I knew he lived across the lake in a rich subdivision and he was maybe a bad boy. I was pretty sure of that. He wasn't a hippie but he wore big glasses with yellow lenses. He had a mischievous look in his eyes. He drove a fancy new fast car and always had a pretty girl with him. I don't remember how it came up, but soon enough we were talking about religion.

The book I was reading, he said, was a Catholic Missal. "Really?" I just remembered the prayers. He had the most beautiful book with him, with a leather cover and thin onion skin pages. He was flipping the pages and reading. I distinctly remember saying to him, "But I'm Jewish. I can't believe in Jesus that way and I don't read the New Testament."

"I'm Jewish too," he said. With a last name like Greenfield, I should have known.

"What if I could show that Jesus was the Messiah, using only the Old Testament?" he asked.

"Well, okay," I said.

I don't remember everything he said, but he spoke with optimism and confidence, two things I was searching for, and, he told me he was certain God loved me. God loved me so much that he sent his only son to die a horrible death for me. I knew about dying horrible deaths! For every point he made, I had a counter and he had a line from the thin onion skin pages for each thing I questioned. One big hurdle was my doubt that Jesus was more than a great man. I knew he was that, but the Son of God?

Another doubt to overcome was this idea that God would care about me. I felt pretty unlovable and insignificant.

Chuck slowed way down and stopped spouting. He stopped the flipping back and forth through the thin onion skin pages and began to read very slowly from the Old Testament.

Isaiah 9:6: "For unto us a child is born, unto us a son is given: and the government shall be upon his shoulder: and his name shall be called Wonderful, Counsellor, The Mighty God, The everlasting Father, The Prince of Peace...."

Isaiah 53:1-5: "Who hath believed our report? And to whom is the arm of the Lord revealed? For he shall grow up before him as a tender plant, and as a root out of dry ground. He hath no form nor comeliness; and when we shall see him, there is no beauty that we should desire him. He is despised and rejected of men; a man of sorrows, and acquainted with grief, and we hid as it were our faces from him; he was despised, and we esteemed him not. Surely, he hath borne our griefs, and carried our sorrows; yet we did esteem him stricken, smitten of God and afflicted. But he was wounded for our transgressions, he was bruised for our iniquities; the chastisement of our peace was upon him; and with his stripes we are healed."

Psalm 22:1: "My God, My God, why hast thou forsaken me?.. all that see me laugh me to scorn: they shoot out the lip, they shake the head saying, He trusted on the Lord that he would deliver him, let him deliver him….I am poured out like water, all my bones are out of joint; my heart is like wax; it is melted in the midst of my bowels. My strength is dried up like a potsherd; and my tongue cleaveth to my jaws; and thou hast brought me unto the dust of death. For days have compassed me: the assembly of the wicked have enclosed me; they pierced my hands and my feet."

Oh my gosh. The Old Testament was talking about Jesus. My heart is breaking. Is this true? Jesus experienced this sorrow, pain and death? Did he really do this for me? This was all foretold in the Old Testament?

In that moment, I believed. I did not understand what that meant or how to say I believed, but I knew that Jesus was more than a man.

Chuck asked me to go with him that evening to some friend's home. I said I'd ask my mom. She didn't ask a lot of questions—she was glad I'd made a friend, a Jewish boy from the rich subdivision across the lake. I hated to admit that I'd go just about anywhere to avoid another night of sitting with death in the VA ward.

I was so nervous when Chuck picked me up in his rich-boy Lotus sports car. It kind of felt like a date, but I didn't like him that way. I hoped that's not what he had in mind.

Sure enough, he just wanted to take me to his friend's home. There were a lot of people there, mostly teenagers with a few adults. It was lively chaos. Everyone was very friendly. There were circles of people talking everywhere and we joined one sitting on the floor. It was the first time I declared I believed. I was forever changed. Suddenly there was new hope budding in my soul, because of my new found belief in life after death. My dad would be going somewhere and I'd be able to join him. For the first time in years, there was hope in my heart.

Little did I know not only how my new faith would change me, but also how this group of people, hugging me and welcoming me, were going to change everything.

Arranged Marriage

There was nothing normal about eleventh grade. In addition to school and daily visits to the VA hospital, there were gatherings almost every night for Bible study. Two years passed and Dad was still hanging on. The days were long and one ran into another. Dad received more release time from the VA hospital and a few day and weekend passes to come home, but this was a very difficult cancer journey. Never once did I hear either of my parents complain. They were gentle, caring and quiet, silently teaching me by example how to gracefully make this journey. Dad endured a lot and Mom and I walked that road with him. It was very difficult for all three of us. The brothers Dad had reached out to, wanting to be close, found it difficult to see and smell Dad's decaying body. They stopped visiting.

Despite the hardship, Mom and Dad encouraged me to spend time away from the hospital to visit with my newfound friends. Several members of the group decided to help my parents. It was really amazing and kind. They made sure my dad was never alone. Someone was there to relieve my mom, taking turns tending to Dad's needs and being encouraging and supportive. They would sit by his bed and read the Bible to him.

The group was growing in numbers. The leader, Ben, preached end-of-the-world evangelism, intensely focused on the teaching of taking up our crosses to follow Jesus. We gathered for our nightly studies at Mimi's house. Mimi was warm and welcoming. She was a boisterous character, with a loud smoker's raspy voice. She was outgoing and not one bit shy, a real ball of energy. She told us how Jesus saved her from a life of fast race horses and fast men. She was 40 years old when she met 43-year-old Ben. He was a hairdresser by trade and didn't own much. They married a short time after meeting. Looking back, it well may have been a marriage of convenience, as I certainly don't remember any display of affection between them. Ben was smooth talking and charismatic. He surrounded himself with teenagers, which seemed to give him confidence. The wayward youths who were converted were encouraged to stay at Mimi's home, leave the world behind and immerse themselves in their faith. Soon that house was full. Ben talked about buying another home and maybe another… and he did. I have no idea how he and Mimi managed financially to purchase homes. His vision was to have one married couple live in each house as its head of household. He needed young married followers.

The intimate time the group members spent with my parents helped with Dad's care and gave him additional companionship along with respite for Mom, as the primary caregiver. The members' service blended into evangelism. For years my parents had not been very religious. Their own journey down a road to death, combined with the charisma of these fervent young converts, led them to a newborn faith. Both my dad and my mom converted from Judaism, accepting Christ as their Messiah and their savior, which I believe brought them genuine peace. At the time, it seemed natural and uneventful, but of course it was huge. Now the door to our home was more open than ever for the followers of this new group to influence my parents.

The group was now called The Way, The Truth and The Life. I had a crush on one of the converts, Louie. He was in his early 20's and had a swagger about him; his conversion saved him from a life of heroin addiction and crime. My parents were alarmed, as I was very naïve. A short time later, Ben came to our home and spoke with my parents. I remember him sitting in our living room on the blue leatherette couch in the one-bedroom condominium. He suggested a marriage for me to Mimi's son, Mickey, who was also a convert from Judaism. They listened, and they gave their consent. Looking back now, I can't imagine why. I was only 17. Maybe they were happy he was Jewish. Maybe it was a relief to them not to have to worry about who I'd end up with. Some 30 years later, my sister speculated that perhaps they felt I would be taken care of, protected from Dad's lengthening cancer and the poverty his death would bring. They gave their consent. It was all arranged.

I did not have a voice. I followed the plan blindly. I had only met Mickey in a group setting, sitting on the floor with others in a circle while he led a Bible study. He was not bad looking and some might even say he was handsome, but he didn't catch my eye. He was not heavy or overweight but not muscular either and he didn't have broad shoulders. We never dated. I was not courted, asked or consulted. It was decided that we would marry and move into one of the houses about to be converted into a commune. A few weeks later, wearing my Sweet 16 dress with white satin on the top, a red bow at the waist and a floral blue and red flower design softly flowing to the floor, in a store-front church at the age of 17, I was married. He was 18 years old and oddly what stood out the most to me was that he was wearing his key ring with hundreds of keys hanging off his belt. He always had that dang key chain hanging off his belt. It would bounce on his hip and make a racket and draw attention to him anytime he entered a room. At least it seemed that way to me. *Why didn't he at least remove it for the ceremony?* I was petrified, horrified and silent.

During the small reception with cake and punch, I was dreading the night. I was a virgin and my mother had merely said, "It'll hurt, but just get through it." That was the only marital advice she ever gave me. I stayed in the bathroom a very long time before finally emerging to find my husband waiting on the bed.

Our first few months of married life we settled into playing house. Ben, who I now thought of as The Leader, moved us and two male "disciples" a few hundred miles away to Fort Myers,

Florida, with the admonition to go out and preach and make disciples. I cooked every meal, every day, and kept the house clean. I felt disconnected, as if I was just observing myself. *God, help me feel comfortable. I don't feel like I'm living in my body.* I was so lonely. I missed my mom and dad. I was only seventeen years old.

Children Having Children

A few months after my marriage The Leader bought a house in North Miami, Florida and sent Mickey and I to live in it to act as heads of household. What did we know about a household? Eight other young disciples moved into the three-bedroom house with us.

Four months into my arranged marriage, I was pregnant with my first child. There was a flurry of fun while Mom helped me get a nursery ready. I was expecting Mom and Dad's first grandchild. We moved the washer and dryer out of the laundry room onto the back porch and began to remodel the laundry room to make a cheerful nursery space. Mom and I searched the carpet stores, driving the alleys looking in the dumpsters for green, white and yellow remnants, because we didn't know if I was having a boy or a girl. We made a patchwork carpet of bright green and other soft baby colors, assembling the squares with electrical tape on the back. This was perhaps the first quilt I ever made. We found a second-hand crib and painted it bright green, buying a new mattress for the bed. My baby shower gift from my parents was a brand-new changing table. It was so special because it was new. My sister gave me 6 dozen cloth diapers—the kind you have to fold so they would last from birth to toddler.

It was a happy space, and yet I was so scared, because I'd never been around babies. Our family had no babies. My only experience with children was at age 15, when I had an after-school babysitting job. A single mother, who was a cocktail waitress with three children, would pick me up after school and take me to her house. I wasn't even comfortable being alone in her house, let alone being responsible for the children. But I got into the routine, fixing dinner for the children, giving them their baths and reading books to them. When their mother got home from work, we'd all load into the car so she could drive me home. That job didn't last long, and it was my only experience with children.

In June of 1972, when I was five months pregnant, with the nursery ready and my belly showing, my father passed away. My baby would have been his first grandchild. There are only a few things I remember about my father's funeral and death. I remember my brothers being horrified that The Leader, Ben, performed the service. I remember there being an open coffin and not going to look. I remember being over-zealous about my new faith and reciting the words I was trained to say with terrible timing, lacking all grace. I remember witnessing about Jesus to my brother Terry and offending him greatly. He was my childhood hero, the one who knew about world religions, and I thought I could tell him, show him and convince him. Perhaps if I had spoken with love rather than just spouting scriptures...perhaps if our father had not just died. It was a conversation I would regret for decades.

When we married, I was not physically attracted to my husband and felt disconnected from him. After all, it was an arranged marriage. I was a virgin when we married and I did not have any confidants, so I thought perhaps the disconnect was normal. Now I was pregnant and we were living in a commune house owned by the cult with four other women and six men. One night, one of the girls who lived in the house told me she had a problem—someone was pilfering through her dresser drawers. I brought this incident to my husband, and that's when he told me. It was him! Since he was three years old, he said, he thought he should have been born a girl. I did not understand what he was telling me. I knew I wanted to run—I wanted out, but I was pregnant and my father just passed away. I was grieving and could not burden my mother with this now. My head was exploding. What was he telling me? He told me that he thought when he accepted Jesus and was born again, he would be a new man and this desire of his would be washed away. He was wrong. He still had urgings and desires to explore his feminine side.

"Absolutely not," I said. He said he would put it aside because of his love for me and his unborn child. He did not want me to leave. That was six months after we were married and we did not speak of it again until the day I found his women's wardrobe, some four years later. Submission silenced my voice. I did not tell a soul.

By August 1972 I was pretty miserable. It's really hot in North Miami, Florida in the summer, especially at seven months' pregnant. We had only one window-unit air conditioner in the house and due to our finances, the rules of the house did not allow me to use it during the day. During my pregnancy I went from being a petite 105 pounds to an absolutely awkward 165 pounds. It was not a pretty picture, nor was it easy to move all that weight around in the heat. In October my beautiful daughter Leah was born. She was 9 ½ pounds and maybe 21 inches long and she was the most beautiful baby ever. Really. I know all mothers say that, but my baby was angelic and so very beautiful. Since I was a group house "mother," I wasn't required to work outside the home, so I was able to be home with Leah. She was easy—happy, healthy, eating and sleeping well. We spent every moment together. If I was cooking or cleaning, she'd be content in her play pen right beside me. If I had to go anywhere, I'd just hold her on my hip and away we'd go. She was my breath, my air.

The night I was in labor with Leah, Ben, the Leader, had a vision of us all living on one remote commune. He set about finding the spot and set us all on the mission of collecting money. We would stand on street corners with coffee cans collecting—no, begging—for our cause. We'd cover neighborhoods knocking door to door with those same coffee cans, asking for donations. That ragamuffin group collected several hundred thousand dollars, enough to buy a little town in North Carolina. It was just north of Marion, near Asheville, on a piece of land bordered by a train track on one side and a beautiful creek on the other. It had a motel, a restaurant and a post office. The motel became housing, the restaurant was

Leah and me, age 18

the dining room and the post office became a sanctuary, decorated with the same patchwork carpeting idea I used in my daughter's nursery. One by one the houses in Florida were sold and everyone moved to North Carolina.

Twenty months after the birth of my daughter, my son Nathan was born. I told the doctors about the large size of my first child. All they saw was one of those commune girls. My due date came and went. I was more than huge. Finally, two weeks past my due date, I went to the doctor and he agreed to induce labor. In those days that meant he gave me a pill and then if that didn't work in two hours, I was to drink a bottle of castor oil. My suitcase was packed. The babysitter was arranged for Leah. I took the pill. In about an hour my labor started. It was hard labor, and it was a 40-minute drive to the hospital. It was a crazy drive through the mountains of North Carolina at high speed with Mickey at the wheel and me standing in the back seat in full-on labor, urging him to hurry and get me to the hospital. When we got there, I immediately asked for drugs to help me. I had been put to sleep for Leah's birth. After examination, they told me it was too late for drugs.

"What do you mean?"

"You're going to have this baby with no drugs!"

Well, truthfully, I don't remember it being horrible. It was fast. My son was born only about 2 ½ hours after I took that pill. He was 9 ½ pounds, just like Leah had been. I do remember being in a lot of pain after the birth. I kept calling the nurses for help. They ignored me. I called again. One of them finally came and said to me, "I don't know how you have babies in the city, but here in the country we don't fuss like you, so settle down."

The next day they discovered the baby had made a large tear in my uterus during delivery and I was bleeding to death internally. I was rushed to emergency surgery to repair the tear, received 8 units of blood and spent another 5 days in the hospital, alone and in silence. My husband did not visit me during those 5 days and I was so sick they wouldn't let me hold Nathan, my beautiful baby. I didn't even get to talk to my mother. Mickey called her to ask her to pray. When we got home my dear commune sisters took care of me and my children. I was very sick for some time. I was jaundiced and ill from the birth, the surgery and the eight units of blood given me for transfusions. After I healed, the doctors said I should not have any more children. I was always uncomfortable with Mickey anyway so now I was grateful for the excuse to refuse sex.

Those first years with Leah and Nathan were amazing. They were happy, comfortable, easy children. They ate well and slept well and I loved being with them every minute. This was one of those silver-lining blessings of the commune. It afforded me the time to just be home with my children. These beautiful babies of mine became my world, my joy, my reason for living and my heart. In 1974, at age twenty, I'd been with the group four years and lived in the commune for three years and had two children. I was still very much a naïve, shy child, but now with children of my own.

Leah and Nathan, 1974

The Early Commune Years

Our commune was based on the grace of God. Salvation is a free gift and cannot be earned. That was the message we heard. That can be in conflict, however, with the teachings of repentance and discipleship. Follow Me. Isn't that what Jesus taught? That literal message was the doctrine of the group: forsake all.

We gathered daily, hearing teachings that warned us of the evils of the world and the doomsday judgment that was sure to be here any moment. The message was blurred and easily distorted for young impressionable followers. The idea that we needed forgiveness and grace was more real because we were reminded daily that we were sinners—horrible sinners. The Bible said so and Ben, our Leader sternly confirmed it. He was charismatic and powerful, his sermons and messages filled with reminders of the devil and hell. He spoke with authority, always with a Bible clutched in his hand.

I was actually falling in love with God. While I could be filled with joy for the gift of grace and forgiveness God showered on me, I was also filled with sadness to think my bad thoughts or deeds added to the reason that God would have to kill his only Son for me. My love of God was shaded with guilt—lots of guilt. The message we received was that we should forsake all and follow Christ to become his disciples and help bring others to the light. There was no thought or teachings that we could be the light *in* the world. We needed to remove ourselves from the world to become new. Young and fervent, we were led into a life of separation from family and the world. It was us and them. It was a message of conflict: forgiveness vs. guilt, love vs. fear.

We memorized scriptures, reading and reciting them over and over again. Most of us were teenagers. It was wonderful to be so immersed in the word. The teachings were lively, detailed Bible lessons woven with history and timelines. The storytelling and discussions painted vivid pictures of the times of the Old Testament and the New. We were learning the Bible, learning about teaching and preaching and how to tell the story of salvation to others. We could not see, then, that we were not just learning; we were being indoctrinated. The scriptures became the only language with which we could communicate. Any questions about our life from outsiders, including parents and family, were responded to only by the repetitious reciting of verses. There was no conversation or communication other than quoting the Bible and scripture. We had no television, no radio and no telephones.

It was a controlled, tactical seclusion. We worked like dogs. In the early days, when we had family homes scattered throughout the North Miami, Florida area, we scrubbed floors, painted houses, cooked and cleaned some more. There was no idle time. There was no rest. The house I lived in shortly after my first child was born, with the laundry room converted into a nursery, had three bedrooms and about fifteen adults. *Crazy.* I stayed home and cooked and cleaned for everyone. They went out and worked. Every night there was sit-down dinner, dessert and Bible study. Others who didn't live in the house would join us. That was the object—bring others in, make disciples—convert souls. We would study scripture and pray until the wee hours of the night, every night, and rise early in the morning, every morning, to do it all over again. The neighbors next to those houses were not pleased with the excessive cars and people gathering on their streets into wee hours of the morning.

When we moved as a group to North Carolina, the transition to further seclusion began. Now there was acreage and facilities to maintain. Between outside jobs, property work, daily Bible studies and parenting, everyone was exhausted. Scheduling our daily lives so full was definitely an intentional form of sleep deprivation. We did not have a choice. We had to participate in the communal chores and the endless Bible studies that were depriving us of our sleep. Our mental state weakened, we were open to manipulation and control. We followed every direction, order and interpretation given us, submitting with blind faith. We were constantly reminded of our worthlessness. Woven into the teachings were reminders that if we were not such bad people, God would not have to punish us. If you broke a glass, you must have sinned. If you got a cold, God was punishing you. If you had a flat tire, God was shaming you. Examine yourself. We were constantly scolded and rebuked. The preaching was filled with reprimand and admonishment. Some might say, but of course, without God we ARE nothing! However, encouraging our formative minds to feel worthless created distress, encouraging deep shame. It is easy to exert power over shamed and distressed youth.

There was a definite hierarchy: cult leader at the very top, deacons next, other men in the group next, and females last. The women or sisters were second-class citizens, in submission to the men. Some people I know still interpret the Bible scriptures in a literal way and find this hierarchy correct. The way it was done in our cult was oppressive and discriminatory. Nothing was open for discussion or debate. If the men said it, then so it was. There were no discussions or arguments because the women were silent; we were told that is what submission meant. We had no voices, no choices. We made no decisions.

Despite all of this, or perhaps because of it, strong friendships were forged and profound life lessons were learned. Woven among the oppression and shame were also some hysterically funny and ridiculous days. The commune in North Carolina lasted for four years. During the first year, my husband and I lived at the main commune property north of Marion in Ashford, North Carolina. We were poor, really poor. Feeding all the disciples took some creative menu ideas. I learned to make a great pot of homemade chicken noodle soup. One chicken makes a huge pot and feeds a crowd. Homemade macaroni and cheese became a favorite. No one even missed the meat. There was a period of time on the main compound that we had to purchase meal tickets in order to eat. The kitchen served as many as 100 people at one time. One meal ticket cost $37 per person, per week and bought one full breakfast, a sack lunch and a full supper including dessert. My husband worked for the commune then and his paycheck was $50 per week. Do the math. We could only afford a single meal ticket meant for one person, but there were four of us sharing the food: my husband, myself and our two toddlers. I remember being hungry a lot that year. I am still famous for my homemade chicken soup, and I love the tricks I learned to save money on groceries, as even now I'm sure I spend way less on groceries than most folks I know.

The main commune took over the town of Ashford and began making headlines in the local newspapers. The children were not in cages, but that is what the local newspaper reported. My husband and I were assigned one of the hotel rooms as our living quarters. Our daughter was one year old and I was very pregnant with our second child. We needed to make our allotted 200 square feet live larger. First, my husband built a loft for our mattress. This allowed us to have the bed raised and underneath it sat a dresser and a rocker. We were getting ready for the new baby. It was not easy climbing up and down the ladder to get to our loft sleeping area, especially at nine months pregnant, when my stomach almost touched the ceiling. Our toddler, however, loved the space. It fit her perfectly. Next, he gutted the walk-in closet. With a clean slate he began to make a children's room. It was a progressive space planning idea. He disassembled the secondhand green crib my mom and I had painted and reassembled it. He was very handy. The crib now had a top on it. He mounted it on the wall at shoulder height. The side of the crib moved up and down for entry into the crib. Treating the mounted crib like a top bunk, he constructed a lower child's bed for our toddler. There was just a short time to get our daughter weaned from crib sleeping into her big girl bed so the crib would be free for the new baby.

This was all done with good intention to make the best use of our space. I have no idea how the local papers heard about this, but the article that was published reported "those people" were keeping their children in cages. There was nothing further from the truth. The newspaper's distortion or misunderstanding of the incident did not make it sensational. The journey was sensational in and of itself.

There was a time when The Leader decided it was appropriate to institute public shaming. If a "sister" committed a sin that warranted such shame, because perhaps she was unrepentant or just needed to be made an example of, then a designated time period was set. The compound had a main road that ran down the center, next to the restaurant that now served as our dining room. There was a line of tree stumps along the road, in front of the dining room, and this is where you sat for a term of public shaming. *Go sit where all can see you have sinned.* I lived with a lot of shame, which is crazy. What did I do wrong? I had not cheated or stolen. I had not committed adultery or killed. I was not a liar. But I did have that secret I was keeping about my husband. *Would God say that was a lie by omission?* I felt ashamed and sinful, and I dreaded the embarrassment of a public shaming. It wasn't until perhaps twenty years later that one of the members told me about how she would intentionally do something wrong so she could be sent to sit on the stump for public shaming. It was her escape from a day of grueling work. I can't believe I wasn't smart enough to think of that myself!

Although our life was secluded, we needed jobs. North Carolina has lots of factories. Some of the folks worked at one that had some kind of chemicals that turned their hair blue. The car would arrive home to the compound and empty out, one by one each person emerging with a head of blue hair. It was odd. Now folks dye their hair for fun: blue, purple, green, or rainbow-colored. I'm not sure of the significance for them, but it always reminds me of hard labor.

Cars were always another issue. It was hard to have a reliable car when we were so poor. We had an old Nash Rambler at one time. The front bench seat was broken and remained in a reclined position all the time. That was mostly an issue because it was a stick shift, four on the floor, and reaching the pedals from a reclining position was difficult for a short person like me. I remember being at a stop light in the hills and having to stand up at the driver's seat to get my feet to the pedals, stomping on the brake and then the clutch to do the dance between the clutch and the gas to get it just right to move forward and not slide back down the hill when the light turned green. I'm sure it was a sight since I was 9 months pregnant behind that wheel! The car was in bad need of a paint job, a luxury we could not afford. We did, however, have a stockpile of Christian Bible verse bumper stickers. My husband used those bumper stickers like wallpaper and covered every inch of the car. Then he mounted a wooden sign to the top of the car (like you'd see on a pizza delivery vehicle). It ran the full length of the roof and had the name of our group on it. Some folks called it the Deacon Mobile. I hated that car. We also had a Mustang for a bit, which put out such a thick billow of black smoke when you took off from a stop sign that it would surely not meet any current emission regulations.

The acreage had a lot of tree work, building and fixing to be done, which kept the men busy. This one time...my husband was with a group trimming trees. Up into the tree he went, inching himself to the exact right spot to be able to reach the intended limb. He sawed it off just fine, except he was standing on it! Then there is the story about a door that didn't fit properly in its frame. They removed the door and trimmed. When they rehung the door, it still didn't fit. It just needed a wee bit more trimmed down. This was done more than several times before someone realized they'd been trimming the wrong end of the door. Oy vey.

We didn't believe that baptism was essential for salvation. We understood that all you had to do was believe. I still feel that way today, but I think baptism is like a wedding: a public declaration. I only remember one baptism in all the years I spent in the commune. We were up in the mountains, by a peaceful pool formed below a spectacular waterfall. A few of the leaders stepped out waist deep into the pool, and one by one we each walked out to them to be gracefully dipped into the waters and declare our discipleship. It's hard to find the words to describe the meaning that day held for me. I had never witnessed a baptism. Why would a Jewish girl know about this type of baptism? I only learned about it from my readings in the commune. That one moment in time was very special for me, as I remember it being all about my relationship with God and the declaration and commitment I declared by my plunge into the water.

Having been on the main commune property for about one year, we were growing. More folks were joining and major improvements were made at the property. In addition to the hotel, which was now housing, we made the hotel lobby a Bible study and prayer center. The restaurant, now the kitchen and dining room, was feeding our members. Above the restaurant was an apartment where Ben, the Leader, lived with his wife Mimi, my husband's mother. My father-in-law was the leader of this cult, but there was no family interaction. The post office became our sanctuary and a printing office. There were houses built and trailers brought on to the property for additional housing. It seemed right that we should grow and expand the ministry, so the Leader, Ben, decided we should have missionary homes scattered about North Carolina. Several homes were purchased. It provided a way for the Leader, Ben, to send away those closest to him, giving him more privacy to do as he wished and more control over those remaining on the main compound.

My husband and I moved to a house in Franklinville, North Carolina, a town with a population of 400. This was to be a mission home about three hours from the main commune property. The house was a three-story plantation mansion on 17 acres with seven bedrooms and three bathrooms. It had a guest house and a graveyard. Eight of us moved into the main house and one couple into the guest house. We hoped to live by the land and be self-sufficient, which meant learning to grow crops and such. This wasn't going to be easy for a bunch of city kids.

We were so poor when we lived there. It was very difficult to feed everyone. I would buy a 50-pound sack of whole wheat. With a hand grinder clamped to the side of the countertop, I would stand for hours cranking. Half the bag would get cracked to use for a porridge. When that cracked wheat was boiled with diced apples, it made a very delicious breakfast. Cranking and grinding the remaining 25 pounds of wheat I made flour for bread making. One pot of soup and several loaves of homemade bread made a delicious and cheap meal feeding 10-15 disciples.

The main compound began to raise pigs. One of the brothers that helped raise the pigs told me his story of when the pigs grew into hogs and it was time to slaughter them. They knew nothing about this. A copy of the *Mother Earth News* was all the instruction they had. They were ready: one had a 22 rifle and the other had a knife. They read they had to shoot it straight between the eyes, while the other guy slit its throat. BAM. The gun went off. Got it. *Mother Earth*, however, had not clarified that they should separate the pigs. When the rifle went off, the other hogs in the pen went wild, charging the guys. Quick—up and over and out of the pen. Oh my gosh. Take a breath and back into the pen. They shot the hog another time and then slit his throat. Whew. Done. Gosh, now how the heck do you butcher a hog? Back to *Mother Earth News*. There was something about a drum and dipping the hog in it. The sketches in *Mother Earth News* on how to butcher a hog left a lot to interpretation and from what I heard their butchering left a lot to be desired.

I don't know whose idea it was that we too should have pigs, but it was suggested we bring a few piglets from the compound property to our Franklinville mission house. Every Sunday we'd load up a station wagon with eight disciples and our two young toddlers and make the three-hour journey to church at the compound. Yes, three hours each way and a day of church and fellowship. It was a crazy long day. It was also good to see everyone. Anyway, now we were to add two more to our journey home. Two pigs that is! A brilliant idea was planned and a crate was mounted to the roof of the station wagon. As we drove down the road the squealing pigs began to... poop. The poop ran down the sides of the station wagon. *What a mess.* I heard laughing, but I don't think it was ours.

We had fig trees in Franklinville, which produced a lot of fruit. It made sense to learn how to make jam and can it. This one day we picked all the ripe figs and mashed them up. They were put in the refrigerator until I could get back to them later that day. Instead, several of the girls went ahead and made the jam. That evening we were having chicken soup. Earlier I prepared the mix so that we could add matzo balls to the soup. An hour before dinner I was going to roll the balls and add them to the soup. I went to look for the bowl of matzo meal and it was nowhere to be found. Turns out the mashed figs were still in the fridge. The girls didn't know the difference and they used the matzo meal to make the jam. We didn't get to have matzo balls in our soup that night. Dinner was thin. Turns out that Matzo Meal with enough sugar makes pretty good jam. We were so naïve.

We planted a few rows of vegetables to grow. One of the neighbors was kind enough to come over and look at our rows. He gave us advice, saying the spacing was not adequate and suggesting that we move some of the rows. The row of green peppers was carefully transplanted, tended and nurtured. We watered and watched the garden grow anxiously waiting for the night we could have stuffed green peppers for dinner. It was months and the plants were big, but no peppers. Turns out we had transplanted the weeds and killed the peppers. Another city kid debacle.

This one time...because my mom had converted and given permission for my arranged marriage, the Leader said it was ok when my mom wanted to come visit. We were in Franklinville at the time and she wanted to see her grandchildren. It was winter and we had no heat. We did have a fireplace, but that big old rambling house needed heat. Each day when she got up, she put on all her clothes, her coat, her gloves and her hat and sat glued in front of the fire. That was her only visit; I didn't see her again for several years. *She had to have been aghast. Thank you, Mom, for always keeping an eye out for me.*

One year turned into two and then into three. I was busy with my children and chores. My husband was always busy with a project to manage or someone to counsel. In those early years he seemed absent from my life. He didn't change a diaper. He didn't help with bottles. I don't recall spending time together as a family unit apart from the group; he was off doing other things. He wasn't harsh or unkind; he just wasn't present. It was OK with me. I loved every minute with my children, and I was still uncomfortable with my husband. My affection had not grown since the day of our arranged marriage. The Bible and the men taught submission and I conformed. I remained disconnected from myself, my husband and from reality.

Discovery

Everyone is gone. The house is quiet. My mind wrestles. I can't do it. Go. I can't do it. The walk to the little house is open and vulnerable. No one has been living in it for a while. On the front porch I stand very still listening for anything—looking for him. Should I go in? He's in town. What if he snuck back here? No, he's in town. Do it.

I turn the knob and step inside the guest house. It has maybe 500 square feet and has a separate bedroom and bath to the left. The kitchen is ahead of me. *I stand very still. My mind is racing. What am I doing here? I'm a very trusting person. I walk into the kitchen and open a few cabinets. Nothing. What did I expect? My legs feel heavy. I walk back into the living area and turn right into the bedroom. There's a closet door on the left. That's it. My mind is at war. There are no words going on but somehow the fear of knowing has consumed me. My heart is racing. I should hurry. Someone might come. I pull open the folding doors.*

Denial and naïveté gone. Disappointment and sadness fill my soul. There are wigs—lots of them. There are shoes—high heeled, bad girl shoes. Now I'm in a rush to see everything. There's make-up and undergarments. It's a full wardrobe of women's clothes in his size. I run out, close the door and hurry back to the house. My mind is on rewind looking for clues—the spaces of unaccounted time, the long, long bathroom time, the plucked eyebrows and shaven chest.

Several months after we were married, he said he had given up his desire to be a woman because of his love for me and our

52

unborn child. He told me that Christ had made him a new man. I was gullible and he took advantage of my youth and naïveté. Now, three years later, I didn't know what to do. Should I tell someone? That is always the question in the minds of women and children who are controlled and wrestle with guilt and shame. It would be so embarrassing. No one would believe me—not about him—a leader in the church—a man's man, a mechanic and such.

I packed a few bags for the children and me. We didn't have much. I waited and waited until hours later when he finally returned. There was no place in the house to talk, with the others home. We walked down the long driveway, alone and quiet. I was not allowed to disobey or question or raise my voice. He was my husband—the authority. I don't remember what I said when I finally got the courage to speak. We were sitting in the van, my head bent over so my hair could hang over my face and hide me. We sat quiet for a very long time before I found my voice. Finally, I told him I found his wardrobe.

I must have told him I was leaving with the children because he was full of remorse and promises. He assured me he'd never do it again. He would pray. He did a. lot of crying and praying, while I wondered what to do. Should I call Mom? It had been a while since I talked to her. Would she believe me? My resolve began to fade. *He seems genuinely sorry. I'm not sure I even know the way from the house to the nearest big city. I can't run away—for better or worse. The Bible says.*

For the next few years, conversations raged in my mind, but only in my mind, as I silently tried to sort out my doubts, fears, feelings and faith. When he looked at me, I felt like he was looking at what he wished he could be. *If he prayed for this desire to be gone and it remains, is it he who is weak or are you failing God?*

He said he went out into the world dressed as a woman. *Did anyone we know see him? Do others know? Do they wonder when they see his plucked eyebrows?*

I looked at everyone differently now, knowing you shouldn't think you know anything about anybody; you don't know what goes on behind closed doors.

I thought that the saying "don't judge a book by its cover" was about not judging someone by the color of their skin or the clothes they wear or the car they drive, but now as I looked at people, I doubted everyone—was anyone really who they represented themselves to be?

There continued to be absences and unaccounted spaces of time in my husband's schedule. I doubted his explanations of what he was doing with his time, but then I'd be certain it was happening. *Who can I trust to tell? What shall I do?* Pray to be able to accept him. My imagination ran wild. *What does he look like when he dresses up? I don't want to know.*

Any thread of connection between us was now severed. He had been unable to put this compulsion aside as he had promised. Why? I'm not sure he even understood it. I certainly had no understanding about his gender identity confusion. The way he carried himself on a daily basis was so masculine, yet he wanted to be female. I did not understand, and I had no way of researching it. He did not talk with me about it, so it was all left to my imagination. I knew some women didn't like ruffles and frilly things. I knew some men liked to wear pink and purple. Obviously, since he had a full woman's wardrobe, he wanted more than a pink or purple shirt. I was trying to accept him just the way he was. Perhaps I could have accepted him easier if he weren't my husband. Perhaps if it wasn't a secret?

The Commune—The Final Years

On one of our weekend trips from our Franklinville mission house to the main compound in Ashford there was something different going on. The ride there was very quiet. When we arrived, the mood in the air was so heavy you could cut it with a knife. There was a group of about eight men with Ben in the motel lobby/Bible study room. I'm not sure of all the exact details and there are different versions. What I do know is that one or two of the young men told a few of the others that Ben had molested them. Someone said, "This is enough." Someone declared, "We cannot continue to allow this behavior."

Before the cult began, Ben had been actively molesting boys and using drugs. He proclaimed that his conversion changed him, but it had not. I think there were a few of the brothers who suspected all along that even back in North Miami, Ben had been taking advantage of the young men in our group and using some of them to procure marijuana and pills. Most of us had no idea that he was still molesting young men and using drugs. I understand forgiveness and new beginnings, but we were children. There was obviously a double standard: we had been programmed to believe that even over-sleeping was a sin punishable by a public shaming.

"No more." They told him he must leave. A few protested, arguing, "He's the last prophet. We can't make him leave!" Ben pleaded. He was finally told that if he didn't leave, they would call the police. With the clothes on his back and a few boxes in the back of his car, he slowly drove away, past the sanctuary, past the restaurant, and past the lodging. He drove away, never to be seen again by most of us.

Word spread fast. "Ben is gone!" A meeting was called in the sanctuary. We were told what Ben had done and that he was gone for good.

What about Mimi, his wife, my mother-in-law? "Did she know? Was she aware?" someone asked. I don't believe she was complicit, but I did wonder. While I had entered the commune as a naïve young child, she had been a woman of the world. I knew something was different about my husband. Wouldn't she have known something was going on with her own husband? She swore she never knew, and at the time I accepted her account.

I don't know all the details. The logistics of dissolving the group was left to the men. I was female—my opinion didn't matter. What I do know is that my husband and I left our mission home in Franklinville and moved back to the main commune property. The decision was made that we needed to leave North Carolina, with a core group staying together. Research was done as to cities and states that might offer affordable living. A few of the men wanted to find a place where they could attend a Bible college and become legitimate Bible scholars, teachers and ministers. People left in pairs, leaving only a small group behind to care for the property and finish up. My husband and I remained among those who stayed; it would be another year before we left the property.

It had been about six years since the day I recognized Jesus as my Messiah and joined The Way, The Truth and the Life. In that time, I was surrounded by many people and, therefore, I had only a very small footprint for myself. I shared a home in the commune houses in North Miami, in the main commune property in North Carolina, and then the mission house in Franklinville. I remained detached in my mind from the brothers and sisters. God also seemed far away much of the time. I did have a few deep and meaningful friendships, but mostly I moved through life in survival mode—indoctrinated, manipulated, and secluded.

I believed God punished us for things we did wrong, and I feared God in a way that kept me at arm's length from both God and people. I was afraid to be too close to anyone, lest they discover how unsure I was about myself and my faith. I wasn't ready for anyone to discover the secret I kept about my husband. As we packed up to move on, my soul was searching and unsure. *How will I navigate the new world I will be living in?* I was filled with uncertainty.

We were children following blindly. Our reasoning and life skills had not been developed. It was a bit more complicated for me since Mimi was my mother-in-law. Although I had never thought of Ben as my father-in-law, Mimi was definitely my mother-in-law. She was a boisterous character, so unlike my mother, who was reserved and genteel. Mimi was a good cook, she loved to draw and she was kind to many. She was very protective and emotionally involved with her son, and very affectionate with him, which was different for me, since my mother didn't show public affection. Mimi and her son, my husband, had an uncanny connection. She didn't think it odd that she would sit on the toilet while he was taking a shower so they could have an extra hour to talk. It didn't seem appropriate to me since we were married, but I never said a word.

The men told us it would take about a year to liquidate everything, so we knew we were going to move somewhere at that time. My friend Rosanne and I decided we'd better think about what kind of job we could get to live *in* the world. There was a technical school in Marion and we applied. In high school my mother had me take typing and shorthand, both of which I was good at and liked, so I enrolled in secretarial courses. It was great fun. We were in the world, riding the mountain roads in her MG convertible with the top down and our waist-length hair flying in the wind. Once we got really brave and snuck off to the movies. We saw "Rocky" and felt free—for a day.

Then my husband said I needed to get a job. I was very anxious. I drove up to Spruce Pine to apply at a blue jean factory, sewing pockets on jeans. I had to pass a dexterity test to be hired. They put me in a room with a 2-way mirror and I sat on the floor with a bunch of wooden blocks. A voice came over the intercom telling me to put the pegs in the appropriate holes. "Ready, set, GO"! Sixty seconds passed. "STOP!" We did several exercises like that for about twenty minutes. Then someone stepped into the room and said, "Thank you very much, but we don't have any openings for you."

"What?" I was stunned. I had failed the dexterity test.

I cried all the way down the mountain because I hadn't found a job, but secretly I was so glad I was not going to have to work in that factory. I stopped at the bottom of the mountain to get a drink at the convenience store. They were looking for help. It was 3rd shift night work, but I applied and was hired on the spot. I could work while my children slept, never missing out on time with them. It was just a relief to get a job. We would have our own money and enough food to eat.

It turned out that this job offered way more than money. I was surrounded by folks who were "of the world," outside the commune. I was out amongst them. I surprised myself because I was comfortable. I worked there for several months, and then one of the vendors asked if he could hire me away. He was a funny little guy, maybe 5 feet tall, with a lot of energy. He ran a kitchen at one of the local factories and he owned three sandwich trucks, a.k.a. roach coaches. He wanted me to drive a route with one of the sandwich trucks. I accepted. It would be day work. I went to the factory kitchen at 5 a.m. to load the truck with food and drinks so I could be at my first stop by 6 a.m. I visited the various factories for break time. I'd pull up and open the sides of the truck, revealing fresh sandwiches, apples and bananas, and fried pies and honey buns and there I stood with my changer belt filled with coins selling my food and offering a smile. My boss was always happy if my truck had a good sale day. My route was done and the truck cleaned and put up by 1 p.m. so I was home by 2 p.m. I liked that job. Off on my own, my thoughts could wander. It was good to not be isolated for at least a few hours each day. I was acclimating myself to the world and to conversation that wasn't a repetition of memorized verses, and I was earning money. Not only that, I was having fun. It was good to be busy. The anticipation of a new future pushed to the farthest recesses of my mind my fear and worry about whether anyone ever saw my husband dressed as a woman.

Finally, a decision was made and revealed—we were moving to Dallas. There was a seminary school there. The Texas economy was good and it was far enough away from our original commune roots in Florida to be different. It would be a fresh start for a future with new beginnings. A small group, of about twenty of us young folks, moved to Dallas. Once there, the leaders realized it was time for everyone to find other churches, other folks—to blend in. We were still so young and inexperienced, and there was a lot of catching up to do. We had been confined without televisions or radios. We had little news of current events. We each had our own personal tragedies and life events that we had missed while we were sequestered in the mountains. We also needed to come to terms with the changes in America. Jimmy Carter was President. What was Watergate? We had missed best-seller books like *I'm Ok—You're Ok*. There were social changes happening. Women were gaining headway in their claims for equal rights.

When I look back at myself in those years, I see a girl that was afraid of her shadow. I was rough around the edges and harsh to some of those around me. I believed that when bad things happened it was God punishing us. I was often abrupt in assigning chores and tasks and remained detached and matter-of-fact. There was no malice in my heart toward anyone, but I know there were times when I was hurtful and unkind, acting without empathy. I was wrapped up in my own survival and fear. I am deeply sorry for the folks I hurt.

We survived an unimaginable time together and some of our connections would remain strong forever. We went our separate ways looking for a light to lead us after being lost at sea. This would be a time to heal, a time to grow and develop a mature relationship with God. I needed to learn that to fear God is not to be afraid, but to have respect.

A Different Way

The seven years of religious commune and being removed from society with no TV, no radio, no communication with my siblings or anyone that did not live in the cult-style commune, made it very difficult to relate to society. The commune broke up, but my mind was still processing everything, with radical submission and actions fueled from fear. I knew there had to be a different way.

We left the commune and moved to Texas in 1978 with the plan that my husband would get the worldly requirements for preaching by attending Dallas Bible Theological Institute. We were able to tell my mom and she came to our aid. She left her secure job and life in California and bought a townhouse in Garland, a suburb of Dallas, so that upon our arrival we'd have a place to land and get our feet on the ground. She helped several families as they reentered society, providing lodging, food and warm loving hugs. When we arrived at her townhouse, she was so happy for the precious time to get to know her grandchildren, who had been secluded in the North Carolina mountains.

My husband got a job at a local car dealer and I got a secretarial job with an insurance company. Mom was so kind; she didn't ask a lot of questions. She cooked and made sure there was dinner every evening. She and I and the children would have family dinner every night. Sometimes my husband would show up, but most often not. Mom actually made friends with my husband's mother, Mimi, who hadn't stayed with Ben. They were both single women with a common thread of children and grandchildren. Mom landed a good job in the area. I don't remember which one came first, but she worked for a while with the Hunt Oil family and also worked for Sun Oil Company.

We settled in. We arrived in Texas in the dead of winter, but spring came and now it was summer. The townhouse complex had a swimming pool, the first my children had ever seen. I taught them to swim in that pool. I felt so at home in the water, splashing and laughing. Being in the pool reminded me of my best childhood years, when I was in the pool in the backyard swimming like a fish; and now, I was teaching my own children to swim.

One night I was looking for some paperwork we needed. Once again, my husband wasn't home yet and so I thought nothing of searching the dresser drawers in our bedroom. I found a packet of pills and some literature on hormone therapy. We didn't have a computer back then so I couldn't Google what this meant. I waited for my husband to get home and tell me but I knew. I waited patiently and silently. I didn't talk to my mother. When he arrived home, I was waiting in our bedroom with the sleeve of pills in my lap. He knew he'd been discovered again. He told me he was investigating his childhood dream. He'd always thought he should have been born a woman, and he was taking birth control pills in hopes of growing breasts. This isn't "normal," I thought. *What is "normal"?* Not a word came from my mouth. All the years of living in a whisper had silenced my voice. Although my mother was in the other room, and I could have talked to her, I stayed silent.

Over the next few days, the internal voices battled. *What God has put together, let no man put asunder. Surely, if God knew this, He would understand that this was too much for me. My husband still wants to be a woman.* During the six years of our marriage, there had been incidents and clues that let me know he was exploring this part of his personality. I reviewed the years in my mind, reminding myself that he didn't tell me about the desires of his heart until after we were married and then only because I discovered the women's clothes in our bedroom dresser that were not mine. All those years ago he had told me that his conversion to Christ made him a new man and that he no longer had those desires. He lied. This time was different. The old, dried film over my eyes was beginning to clear.

I whispered, asking him to move out. He refused, somehow convincing me that this latest exploration of his was caused by the stress of living with my mother. If we got our own apartment where he could act more like a man, be the head of the household, we'd be OK. I believed him at some level. Maybe I knew I needed to give him one last chance.

After all my mother had done for us, leaving her secure position in California, relocating and buying a home in Dallas with enough room for us, we left her place without an explanation. It must have broken her heart. I did not know how to explain. She had to have known we were not happy. Mickey showed up every night very late, always with some tale of a mishap that had delayed him. I was sullen and quiet.

We found an apartment only a few miles from my mother. It was nice enough and we set up house. My husband was selling cars and I was still working as a secretary. The children went to day care. We were living a "normal" life. We'd go to work and come home. I'd get home first and have precious time with the children for stories and baths while we waited for Dad to get home. He would set the time for our dinner and then arrive home hours late, always with some excuse. Having our own apartment had not changed anything, other than giving him more time for which he did not have to account. I also had more time to sort out the voices in my head. *What are my choices?*

When I called my sister with distress in my voice, she told me to ask Mom to help with babysitting and just get myself to the air-port—a ticket to her town in northern California would be waiting for me. I called Mom and packed in a hurry. Leaving a brief note for my husband with little explanation, I was off.

For several days I just stayed in the guest room at my sister's house, unable to sort through the confusion swirling in my mind. I was exhausted mentally and physically. I was so withdrawn and removed from reality, lost and unsure of how to find my way out of the dark. When I emerged, I was ready to confront the unknown. My brother-in-law was an artist and he suggested I start by painting a mental picture of the dream for myself and my children. "Any work of art will be expensive," he said, "but if the beholder sees its beauty, it will be worth the price."

Using words instead of paint, I began. First, there were just outlines shaded with broad ideas. The picture began with the children. They were starting school, maybe riding a bus. There was a swing set for them to play on while I was cooking dinner. There was a fence and a garden. We went to the zoo. It was quiet and peaceful, with water in the scene. The hard work to pay the price for that picture would be worth it. There was no place in the painting for my husband.

So how will I be able to have that picture?

As I left California and headed back to Texas, I was resolved to find a way to get that picture. My sister hugged me tight, willing me her strength, and put a $1,000 check in my hand to be used, if need be, to help me buy the picture—a fresh start, a new life.

The plane ride home was full of anticipation. I got to the apartment and waited for my husband to arrive. I had to summon the strength to shut out the voices in my head that were still yelling *submit, submit, submit.*

Stand up for us! He must leave. Given the manipulation he had used for years, this would be very difficult to accomplish. My anxiety built as I waited. There had been several times over the years when I told him I wanted to call our marriage quits, but never did I have a plan or strong ground to stand on. Now it was different.

He must leave, I told him. He had to go.

He refused. He said I could leave if I wanted, but he was not leaving.

"Don't try to take the children," he declared. "If you do, I'll take them underground and you will never see them again." I believed him. The net of submission was going to be very hard to escape. *What should I do?*

He kept telling me he loved me. He desired me. I was the desire of his heart. But I knew now that I was just what he wished he could be. He wasn't loving me—he was looking through me. I had always been uncomfortable with him. I thought it was me. I was so naïve when we married. I never dated and had no idea about intimacy. My parents were not publicly affectionate. How were a woman and a man supposed to act together? How should I feel as a woman?

I thought the problems between us were my fault; it was because I was immature and didn't know how a woman should be. I thought I'd ask his permission, but instead I came out with a declaration. I found my voice and whispered, "I must sleep with a man who feels all man so I can know if I feel like a woman."

That was the only way to save our marriage, I thought.

"I forbid you," he said.

He saw no reason that his wanting to be a woman should end our marriage.

No Do Overs

When my husband refused to leave, I sought professional advice. The counselor said I should just learn to deal with the fact that he wished he was a woman. But the counselor did not live in my skin. The dialogue going on in my mind was getting louder and louder.

A little time had passed since the restricted days of the commune and I was maturing. I knew I needed space to gather positive thoughts of strength and resolve. I had to get him to leave. *Can I support the children and myself?* Could I do it with only a GED and $450/month income? I had to think. I needed to dig deep. I was still insecure, submissive and silent.

I also did not feel that I could tell family or friends that my husband wished he was a woman, even though there was a voice in my head screaming, "He is not who he says he is." My soul was in pain and my heart was breaking. I sought more advice, this time from an attorney. I did not tell him about my husband wishing he was a woman. No one knew. No one would guess. He was a leader in his church. He worked on cars and had a very male persona. The attorney told me that if there was an "agreed-upon separation," even if I was the one who left, a court could not accuse me of abandoning my children.

When he arrived home that night, I asked him once again to leave. He refused. I was finding my voice and now I had a job and the $1,000 my sister loaned me. I was definitely afraid, but I knew I needed to have a little time where I did not see him daily so that my thoughts could get back to focusing on the beautiful picture I was painting that I had dreamed and envisioned of me and my children building a life.

The corners of my mind were filled with doubt and fear, leaving no safe place. My mind had been brainwashed in the commune and my thoughts were at war, with my every thought met with the reciting of a verse. The verses streamed endlessly in my mind, filling me with guilt and submission. I felt worthless and incompetent. How can I even contemplate what I'm thinking? I wasn't sure I could care for myself. I left home for this arranged marriage as a child. Spending all those years sequestered in the mountains with no outside communications kept me naïve. It was a good tactic on the part of the cult leader. All those years I heard the message that because I was a sinner and weak. Jesus died for me and while that humbled me and gave me hope for eternal life, the way the message was delivered encouraged enormous shame and weakness, especially for a woman. I was silent during my childhood. I was silent at my father's side in the VA hospital. I was silent in the commune. I was silent with my husband's secret. The silence was deafening.

The battles raged in my mind and soul. I could barely stand to be in the same room with the man who wished he was me. Still in silence, one day in 1978, I concluded I had to leave. I am crying as I write this. I must dig very deep to try and explain, but the words are never enough. I will try.

I thought I was only leaving for a short time. It breaks my heart even today to tell it. I saw no other way and I left. I had to save myself to save my children. Yes, I left alone. It was the best and the worst decision of my life. I could liken it to surviving a fire. When my mother was sixteen, she was in a horrible car accident. When the car rolled it pinned her in. While she waited for help, hot oil or gasoline poured over her body. She survived, but she bore large scars over her body from it. I did not mean for my departure to be permanent. I truly thought I'd sort it out in a month or so. I thought my husband would realize that we had to split and the children would come to live with me. That is not how it happened.

It was horrible. I missed my children. I struggled with thoughts of going back, but I knew that I had to find my voice, my strength and peace. I was only 24 years old and already I had survived paralyzing polio, crippling childhood shyness, a four-year quiet journey of death with my dad and then seven years of a sequestered existence in the commune. I wasn't sure I could survive this. I was scared and I was still silent. I had to find my voice. I was so young. I did see the children often. My daughter was just starting kindergarten. They seemed OK. I cried a river almost every day. And I did three things without permission: I smoked my first cigarette, had my first alcoholic drink and cut my hair.

It didn't take very long for me to realize that I didn't ever want to live with my husband again. I talked to him again about the children living with me. He said he could afford private schools for them and was buying a big house where they could grow up. His family and the children's cousins would live nearby. He was doing quite well financially, selling cars and running a transmission shop. How could my apartment living and public schools compete with that? He reiterated he'd never give up custody. He reminded me that if I even tried, he'd run and take the kids underground so I'd never see them again. "Face it," he said. "You left. You are never getting them."

Submission, guilt and terrible grief filled my soul, along with self-hatred. He was right. I was not strong enough.

My whole life up until then had been filled with silence. Some people would even say I was sullen. It was as if I was living in a silent movie. I was silent for my arranged marriage. I was silent about my husband wanting to be a woman. I was silent when he took my children. Did I even have a voice?

I believe that the decision I made to leave alone was necessary for the survival of my core self. The separation from my children was indescribably painful. There are no words to describe the devastating pain and shame. And the silence was replaced with more secrets. When asked why my husband and I split I didn't feel I could say because he wants to be a woman. I used to chuckle and say I got divorced because I got tired of waiting, because he was late all the time. His femininity had to be a secret. My voice was not mature enough to speak those words.

The first few reactions to me being a mother without custody taught me that now I had another secret. People would ask about my children. Where did they go to school? As they realized they did not live with me, the expression on their faces showed harsh judgment, assuming I must be unfit. More shame for me to carry as the stigma began to define me, because I could not adequately explain how this happened. I was called selfish and weak. One person said I lost my salvation and was going to hell. The biggest problem was not how people reacted and what they said, but that I believed all that about myself. Somehow, I survived the worst trauma of my life caused by my leaving and becoming a mother without custody.

Visitation times were standard. Every other weekend the children were with me and one week night we had dinner together. We would cook and bake and play card games like Fish and War. We had one of the first video games on the market called Burger Time. I don't recall being invited to attend and participate in the children's school activities. I'm sure they always wondered why I didn't attend. Interacting with the school and other parents would lead to lies. I wasn't sure if I was around my ex-husband, who would be at those events, could I maintain the secret? I missed out on so much. While he had been absent from our marriage, he did seem like he was there now for the children. Shortly after I left, he took a new wife. She was beautiful and kind to the children and to me. It amplified to me that I was the one in the wrong to leave. To the world there was nothing wrong with him.

At that time, I was not able to cope with the harsh judgments and the shame of being a mother without custody. Even the questions were too painful. All these years later, as I write this, I can't believe I did not imagine the depth of the pain and how that choice would affect everything. In the 1960's divorce rates surged. In the 1970's, some courts were beginning to entertain the question of what would be in the best interest of the children involved. I thought about my lonely childhood and I wanted something different for my children. The idea that they would have extended family around them gave me some form of comfort. I was hoping not only for my survival but for theirs. This was uncharted territory. It would be different, but I thought we could adapt and create something new out of this situation. I reminded myself that I didn't do anything wrong. *I am not unfit.*

I still live with the stigma and the scars. *Some roads we choose are one-way. Sometimes there are no do-overs.*

PART TWO

Good Girls Go To Heaven

Polio numbed my legs for two years. When I was able to walk, my parents discouraged any physical activity other than swimming. That, combined with our constant moving and the "Hollywood Years," made for a solitary childhood. As a child I tried to make friends. Around age nine I struck up a friendship with a girl a few years older than me. She was one of seven sisters and brothers and her house was always a beehive of activity. My parents were so happy I'd made a friend; they never asked any questions about her or her family. She had a pool in her backyard, and we would swim a lot.

Some days the two of us would catch the city bus and ride the 10 miles from Van Nuys to Reseda all by ourselves. It wasn't odd back then. We'd go to the drug store and look at make-up and have a soda at the counter. We'd buy great big family-size candy bars and go to the movies. We'd spend all day together alone and then ride the bus home. I was still a young eleven, while she was a mature thirteen. Her body was fully developed. Mine, not so much. She loved parading her new shape. I was inhibited. She was daring and experimenting. I was only observing. She was trying alcohol and cigarettes and boys. It was the 60's, in California. She was free. I was uncomfortable, hearing my mother's voice of disapproval. I was a good girl. She was, well, maybe not. We tried to stay friends through more moves, but we grew apart as our differences grew.

Around age thirteen, at a new school, I was introduced to a new group of kids who were definitely living on the edge. In California in 1967 you could not tell a book by its cover. My folks would have been horrified if they had really known these kids. "You get the reputation of the people you hang around with," my mother would say. At every gathering this group was experimenting with alcohol, sex, drugs and rock n' roll. I was out of my element and I knew it. I did not participate in the alcohol, sex or drugs, but I did buy a few rock n' roll albums. I'd listen to Cream or Led Zepplin, but I didn't like it. I preferred Johnny Mathis or Frank Sinatra. When I was with my new friends, I kept to myself and just made sure they got home safe; I was glad to be included in the group.

By age fifteen, I had my one and only teenage date. Although I had seen a lot by now, I was still very naïve and terribly shy. It was harmless and boring. He was a nice Jewish boy, the son of a friend of my parents. It was a car date, alone with him, but it was uneventful and harmless.

Then at sixteen I met the group from the religious commune. The years in the commune were like an out-of-body experience, where it seemed like I was observing, not participating. The separation from my family and much of society fueled my introverted nature. While I had some meaningful relationships, I still felt like an outsider and uncomfortable. My mind and body were not in sync.

I could feel my legs now, but I was still numb inside. The stage had been set by my lonesome and frail childhood, followed by the cult years, and then the shock of my husband's declaration that he wanted to be a woman and the profound grief of losing my children. I was at a crossroads. I was in a fight for my life to break out of the silence that had dominated me. I needed to learn to stand again. To stand up for myself. *Who am I? No, who do I want to be?*

I thought if I tried new things, I'd feel something. In reality, I was setting off on a path that called more than ever for my mind and body to live separately. It would be hard to survive the single years. I thought, I've tried heaven, now I think I'll try hell. Perhaps I didn't exactly formulate that precise of an intention, but remember I cut my waist-length long hair, lit my first cigarette and had my first taste of alcohol. Perhaps all things were possible.

While I knew I must live without my husband, I did not envision that he would take my children. The grief was immeasurable. Now my soul was numb. With a careless abandon for the first time, I was determined to break the silence and to learn to feel. I wanted to feel music and energy. I wanted to feel beautiful and loved. I wanted to feel free and to feel like a woman.

All my life I played by the rules, most of which were centered around control. *Don't cry.* My mother didn't like for us to cry. We really were not allowed to cry. Modeling school taught me to focus on my walk so that there would be no evidence of my disability. I had to hide my feelings; I had to hide my physical imperfections. I know that my mother was trying to encourage me to be strong. *You can do anything. Nothing can hold you down. Be positive. We have it so much better than so many others*—and we did. But the take-away was also that I should hide *myself*—whoever that was?

Silence does not always equal peace. Silence was a mask hiding many emotions, including anger, fear, self-hatred, doubt and shame. Silence also masked my insecurity and the fact that I didn't really know how I felt about so many things, but mostly about myself. After seven years of committed devotion to God, following what I believed to be God's call to forsake everything and everyone of the "world," now I was alone and confused. I was mad at God. I didn't want Him to walk beside me anymore. I wanted to try this on my own. I was reacting and blaming, using my loss to fuel my justification for the path I was choosing.

One feeling that out-weighed loss was shame. With the endless reels of indoctrination still running in my head, I felt shame for everything. As I review my young life, I recall that as a child I felt that I was a burden on my family. When I joined the commune, I left my mother to care alone for my dying father. I was not strong enough to speak up for myself. I was not strong enough to fight for my children. I was so ashamed of myself. I was a weak human being. I was afraid of God. I was alone.

Then I heard disco. The nightclubs were filled with songs like

I Wanna Dance with Somebody by Whitney Houston and *Sexual Healing* by Marvin Gaye. The music was energetic and had rhythm. I discovered that I liked the tone of the blues, which spoke to my sorrowful soul. There were discos up and down Greenville Avenue in Dallas and Tuesday night was ladies' night. Drinks were a quarter. Alcohol was new to me...the taste, the various concoctions and the effects. Some nights every round would be a different drink—just to try. There were screwdrivers and margaritas, wine coolers and spritzers, Bloody Mary's, B-52 shooters and Colorado Bulldogs, the sweet hazelnut of Frangelico and finally Scotch on the rocks—extra rocks please. The music and the alcohol drowned out the voices in my head, but only briefly. The dancing gave me an energy I didn't know I had. Hours and hours of drinking and dancing gave me false confidence.

I was looking for love in all the wrong places and in all the wrong faces. I put myself in dangerous and unspeakable situations without any regard for my safety whatsoever. What did any of it matter? I felt alive in the moment. I was so lonely from the loss of my children and the loss of my trust. Perhaps it should not have been such a loss that the father of my children wished he was a woman, but his desire affected my ability to trust anyone. I was shaken to the core and now I doubted everyone I encountered. I didn't trust men. I didn't trust my faith. I didn't trust my God and I didn't trust myself.

In the disco, though, with the lights and music and drink, it didn't matter who I was with. I had no regard for them or for myself. I was in the fast lane on this road to hell.

Big Daddy

Alone, with little money, I tried to survive not only the loneliness, but the hunger and the voices. I knew I had to get a better job. I was working as a secretary in a small insurance office. I never told anyone, but sometimes the boss would lock the office door and take advantage of me. I did not speak up for myself. I felt more shame and totally powerless. I still had no voice and lived under submission, now to him. I knew I had to break free yet again. Every Sunday I spent the money for a newspaper so I could read the "Want Ads."

There was an advertisement for a job at a film company in Dallas, Texas. Who knew there was filming and the world of Hollywood in Dallas? I applied. I went for all kinds of testing, written and verbal, and multiple meetings with managers and even the owners. It was a huge raise when I went to work for Victor Duncan. I was free from the abuse at my insurance company and got a huge raise by making the move, $610 a month to $850 a month. But after I had been there about eight months, I started to question whether I belonged in Dallas. My children were there, and I lived for the times when we were together, even though we didn't do anything extraordinary. And I had met a man, Steve, with whom I felt chemistry and promise. But I thought perhaps a change of scenery or a more familiar place would help me feel more at home. My mother had since moved back to California. There was a dear commune friend in Florida, who invited me to join her there. I packed all my belongings in my beat-up orange Volkswagen Beetle Bug and emptied out my checking account. It took me just a few days to get to Florida and spend every cent of all the money I had to my name—$500 gone.

Only a few days after I left Dallas, I knew I had to return because I needed to be where my children were and that was Dallas. And then there was Steve, who called me every day, asking me to come back and give our relationship a chance. My friend Rosanne didn't want me to drive back alone, so she declared it road trip time. She rode with me and helped deliver me safely back to Dallas with only a few mishaps along the way.

Now I needed another job. I applied at a company to drive a sandwich truck. I told them I drove one in North Carolina and that I could load my own truck. I think I had the job before I even told them that. They saw a cute, petite young thing and hired me without much of an interview. I never showed up for work the next day, as I realized I needed a real job, one that would lead somewhere. I decided to apply for secretarial jobs, even though the last one hadn't gone so well.

Call it luck or fate or God watching out for me. What happened next was a miracle. There was an advertisement for a job I just knew I had to answer—they were looking for a secretary with typing and shorthand. I thought, *"That has to be me."* Tom James was a well-established and well-respected litigation attorney, who earned his degree at SMU Law School, attending after already having a family, which was quite an accomplishment. He had been chairman of the Dallas County Republican Party and was friends with men like Herb Kelleher, CEO, the founder of Southwest Airlines, and T. Boone Pickens. He was around 6 feet tall, slender, well-spoken and well-dressed with monogrammed shirts and custom-tailored suits. He was in his 50's when I met him, and engaged to a kind and beautiful Dallas interior decorator. He reminded me a little of my dad. In the interview I boasted about my modest experience. I told him that if I was given the opportunity, I could learn anything and that I'd work very, very hard. He listened like a father would listen—and indeed, he had three daughters all around my age.

Tom would become my mentor and my friend. Reflecting back, it's impossible for me not to attribute meeting Tom James as one of the most important meetings of my life. God surely had a hand in that meeting. Thirty years later, I wrote the following letter to Tom on the occasion of his 80th birthday, to celebrate how far we both had come.

Dear Tom,

It's been 30 years since that June day in 1979 when you advertised for a secretary. The classified ad said 4-days a week. That's all I needed to hear. Jackie ushered me into your warm western office. The moment I walked in I knew I wanted to stay. We visited for a while. Boldly I touted my experience as a roach coach driver. I can take Gregg shorthand at 90 w.p.m. I can type at 90 w.p.m. and I survived a religious commune. What better qualifications could I need? You were listening to my words, but mostly to my heart, and watching me and looking directly in my eyes. You saw a little bit of a bird, with wounded wings, yet a strong will to fly. You scooped me up and took me in and ... changed my life forever.

Things were a little different then. We had that IBM mag card that I just could not figure out. You bought me a computer and...changed my life forever.

We had the sweet smell of your pipe in the office most days. We had lots of cafeteria lunches. I know you just thought I was so frail and were probably afraid that the only meal I ate was the lunch you bought me and so many days you were right. Again, you were listening and looking.

Remember the day I asked if I could borrow your credit card because I wanted to buy a television? You said you'd think about it. Later you told me I'd spoiled the surprise because you were going to give me one for Christmas. We looked at Consumer Reports and then found the best deal and on a cold December day you said, "Come on" and off we went. A short time later, we had the top down on the Karmen Ghia with the huge, really huge, box in the back, riding down the road. Then you lugged that thing up the stairs of my apartment building and set it up for me. I'm not sure who was happier that day.... me, to get a TV or you....to give it to me. That day you wore a Santa hat and the glimmer in your eyes... changed my life forever.

Remember when you decided to make my bonus a vacation? I decided to take a 3-day cruise. At the end of the trip, I called and said I'd be late getting back to the office. Late by one week. You listened and you knew and your gift...changed my life forever.

When I got home, I'm sure I was a babbling idiot. I was a love-sick puppy walking around on cloud 9, but you listened and watched. One day you said, "So—you're gonna marry that sailor, aren't you? Well, the best gift you can give him is to make his children love you." Those wise words were the best gift and... changed my life forever.

I love the way you listen. I love the glimmer in your eye that looks directly at me and through me right into my heart.

One day you began to call me by my childhood nickname. Even now, I can hear you in my head, calling me... Baby Ades. That's when I knew that while you'd been my mentor, my teacher, my Santa, my mama bird, and my friend, you were also my Big Daddy.

There's a saying that sometimes in life, you find a special friend; someone who changes your life just by being part of it. Someone who makes you laugh until you can't stop; someone who makes you believe that there really is good in the world. Someone who convinces you that there really is an unlocked door just waiting for you to open it.

Thank you, Tom James, my Big Daddy, for listening and watching and looking into my eyes and heart and taking a chance. Thank you for making me part of your life and for making me want to be a better person and for being my friend. You changed my life forever.

I love you dearly
Baby Ades

Tom did so much for me. First, he gave me a career in the legal field. When my children needed school clothes, he'd hand me his credit card and tell me to go get what they needed. The VW beetle bug I drove was falling apart. I asked if I could borrow money to get new tires. He said "No, but here's what I'll do." Out came *Consumer Reports.* He bought a brand new Nissan and told me it was the company car, but it was mine to drive. When the note was paid off in five years, if I still worked for him, he'd sign the car over to me. Of course, he lived up to that promise. I never doubted a word he told me. I was learning to trust again.

When he realized I was still having trouble fitting in to the world from the commune days and adjusting to life without custody, he paid for me to see a therapist weekly. What Tom really gave me was belief in myself and he offered his friendship and a listening heart. To this day, his friendship and his influence in my life contribute greatly to who I am and the decisions I make. I am eternally grateful for the pure strong relationship we share.

Single Years

The 1980's were progressive. Ronald Regan was elected and Pac Man was released. Charles and Diana were married and Microsoft released Word. Yuppies, or young urban professionals, focused on corporate jobs and shiny objects. There were whispers in the news of the deadly disease AIDS, Acquired Immune Deficiency Syndrome.

I focused on learning my new legal secretary job by day, while at night I was learning to drown haunting voices with music. I spent a year with Steve, the musician. He was my first love. We talked about a future, but my soul was still very restless and he wanted children. I could not have more children. The doctors told me after the birth of my son that I should not get pregnant again, since he was delivered naturally and weighed 9.5 pounds, and he made a few tears on the way out. The doctors said—no more risks. No more babies. My heart could not even consider adoption. How could I explain to my children why they couldn't live with me but a new child would? I just couldn't do it and so I did everything to wreck the relationship with Steve. I couldn't drown out the voices totally, but the music helped.

West Coast Swing, also known as Push, was on the dance floors in Dallas. I always dreamed of learning to dance. As a child I loved all the musicals and I had rhythm. I couldn't believe that this girl, who had never been allowed to participate in sports as a child, protecting and preserving my precious legs and energy, was learning to dance. Look at me! I'm dancing! Days filled with work. Nights filled with music and dancing and strangers.

The children were with me every other weekend. They were adjusting well, having a positive childhood. They had cousins in their life. They had their grandmother, Mimi, doting on them, and before my mother moved back to California, she enjoyed spending time with them too. They were in private Christian school, and their step-mother was an angel. She was the rock and the strong person in the lives of the children. Their dad was absent again, but she was there. We treated each other with respect and kept the children's best interest at heart. We made the effort to be more than civil, knowing it was our responsibility to keep any adult tension away from the children. When the children were with me, our times together were happy; we'd swim and play games and cook. Only then did the voices in my head stay quiet, leaving me alone. Otherwise, shame and guilt covered me like a heavy wool quilt on a hot summer day.

During this time of my life, I didn't want God to walk with me or watch over me. Someone told me that He was always on my shoulder, right there next to me. I took my hand and brushed Him away. I said I didn't want to take Him to the disco. Little did I know it was not that easy to separate from God.

In those early single years, I met Kathy, who would become my best friend and my designated everything. We met when I worked at the insurance office. We were told we could pass for sisters, and we do look a lot alike. I was still married when I met her, but on the verge of divorce. She was newly divorced. I had two children. She had one. When we started spending time together, she quickly became my best friend. She taught me about a budget and helped me manage my money as I lived paycheck to paycheck. We found out we both liked crafting and reading and dancing. When I was younger, I had been the one helping others to get home safe. Perhaps I was paying that forward. Now I had Kathy in my life, who always made sure I got home safe. She was the keeper of my secrets, and to this day she is still my strong ally and confidant. She is an anchor for me in time of storms and a cheerleader for me when things turn out right. She was my first adult female friend not from the commune. I felt I could be myself with her, whoever that was. We went to Austin together for a weekend and found we were also compatible as travel partners. She was grounded and responsible and funny and caring. Our relationship was a reminder to me of the amazing strength derived from women's friendships.

Time marched on and I was feeling settled into this new life of mine. I loved my wonderful job with Tom James. In his upscale, elite law office I dressed for work every day wearing suits and hose. I loved to dress up. It felt dignified. My days felt a bit like an episode from Perry Mason. I also loved my growing friendship with my dear friend Kathy. It was going on five years that I was single and while I missed my children living with me, I realized that I was quite comfortable living on my own.

Love of My Life

This one time...my boss Tom said, "You have a big birthday coming round. How about if you take a vacation for your bonus?" My friend Kathy and I started planning how we would bring in a new decade in style. Our thirties were approaching. We decided we'd fly to Florida and spend a week with friends at their time-share condo on Fort Lauderdale beach and then take a three-day cruise to the Bahamas. We were so excited for the adventure of sun and fun.

The time-share was fabulous, right on the beach. It was a revolving door of people. Rosanne and Chuck actually lived in Fort Lauderdale so their friends and family were in and out. Rosanne and I each survived our own journeys in the commune and were glad for the much-needed time to catch up and reconnect. My two forever friends, Kathy and Ro, all together! Triple trouble, full of frolic and fun. We were wound up and excited to be independent women, visiting with plenty of pool and beach time. Though we didn't sleep much in seven days, we did party! Boy, did we party. I remember a yacht, dancing, and a crazy wild time.

Then it was time for Part Two: boarding our cruise ship. Oh my gosh—a cruise! My parents loved to cruise; this was going to be my first. She was an older ship called the *Emerald Seas*, carrying 1,200 passengers and 412 crew. Once on board, Kathy and I started counting our money, literally; we sat on the bed in our cabin counting out dollar bills, realizing that we'd barely have enough. The ship was on a cash basis and we had to cover all the drinks, tips and activities.

Ready, set, bon voyage. The *Emerald Seas* was an old girl, small and personal. We found our cabin and began to explore. It was lively and enticing—the slots, the music, the people and the adventure. At dinnertime we changed and put on our party attire. We roamed, finding our way to cocktail hour and dinner. We noticed the men in uniforms here and there and that added to the buzz of the ship. There was a mixer for singles, which was quite reserved, stately, and nice. The next night was the formal captain's welcome aboard party. We made sure to be there for the free cocktails and to see the officers up close. They were from Greece and looked like gods. They were so darn handsome!

At dinner that night Kathy had been having fun flirting with our adorable waiter, and they made a date to meet the next day for sun and fun on the private island, Little Stirrup Cay, owned by the cruise line. She was excited to have a date for the day. As the evening progressed, we explored every nook and cranny of the ship and every bar. We finally landed in a spot with a dance floor and a group of officers at a table across the room. An officer strutted over and asked Kathy to dance. Kathy and I and the officers talked and danced and, well, we were having a grand ole time. *Whoosh. Take a breath, Adrienne.*

It was getting late. I turned to Kathy and said, "Look at the quiet man in the corner sitting at the table with the officers. I think all these officers work for him. He's the one we should be getting to know."

We said our good nights and as we were leaving, the boss man said, "If you're going to Little Stirrup Cay tomorrow, maybe I'll see you there."

"That would be nice."

We got out of their earshot and Kathy whispered, "Oh my gosh. I made that date to meet the waiter at the island and now the boss wants to meet us. What are we gonna do?"

"Follow me," I said. One of the qualities of the wonderful special friendship I have with Kathy is that we share the lead, volleying it like a ball. As we headed to guest services, I asked her to give me the handwritten note the waiter had given her. Perhaps a little bit tipsy, I leaned into the purser behind the counter and said, "It's urgent. We need help." Pretending to be Kathy I continued, "I made a date with our waiter for the beach tomorrow and now I don't know how to reach him to say I can't make it." I showed her the note. Cruising in those days was so different. Everyone knew everyone. She knew who had given us the note. I wrote a note of regret, signed Kathy's name and gave it to the clerk who said she'd make sure he got it. As we left the desk, Kathy said, "Thank you, thank you, thank you!" And I said, "Well thank goodness we'll never see these people again!"

The next morning, we were excited for our day at the private beach island. We got to the shore and strolled all around before we spotted the boss man, Oscar, with a few of the crew. We were invited to join their group. It was a marvelous day. We were in and out of the ocean, lots of relaxing sun and a lot of Pina Coladas. When we left the island there was no plan made for seeing each other that night. It was just a really nice day.

The ship that night was a ball of energy, or maybe that was just me. It was our last night of the cruise, well—of our whole vacation. It had been awesome and fabulous. We danced. We drank and roamed and spent time in each bar and then the disco. Each night the officers would spend time in the disco, adding to the energy and ambiance. What a night!

When Kathy decided to go to bed, I was still in the mood to roam the ship. I didn't want it to end. I wanted to linger a little more and said I'd be along soon. I just wanted to feel the ship, soak her in before we'd have to say goodbye in the morning. I loved the sound of the ocean and the slight movement of the ship on the water. As I strolled the deck, I felt like I was in paradise, with the deep blue sea all around and the night sky above. On my last circle around the deck, I saw him sitting there, at a table by himself. "Hi Oscar," I said. "May I join you?"

We talked and talked and talked about the places we'd been and the places we wanted to go. He was interesting and adventurous,

Me, Oscar and Kathy on the *Emerald Seas*, 1984

real and mature. The night sky, the sound of the ocean and the conversation were intoxicating and seductive. *I like this man*. It was the wee hours of the morning before we began to move slowly toward our cabins. We didn't want to leave each other's company. There wasn't much time before we disembarked, and we decided to spend those last few hours together. At 8 a.m. he asked if he could take Kathy and me to the airport for a few more stolen minutes. At the airport Oscar said to me, "It's a shame you can't just stay and sail some more with me so we could get to know each other better. I'm not ready for you to go."

I excused myself, found a public telephone and called my boss to say I would not be coming back for another week. Then I called my Mom. I took Kathy aside and said, "I think I need to stay." She agreed. Giddy, I went back to Oscar and announced, "I'm ready."

There was a very long pause, then a moment of panic in his

eyes, and finally he found his voice and said, "Well, I better make some calls." There was no available cabin on the ship; it was fully booked. But the chief engineer was on vacation, so they prepared his suite for us. We explored the ship hand in hand. It was so magical and romantic.

Two days later, strolling down the streets in Nassau, he bought me a gold anchor charm, which carries with it the superstition that the owner will return to the place it was obtained. Holding hands and strolling, without missing a beat or looking at me, Oscar said, "This is what it would be like to be on a honeymoon with me." He was so handsome to me, with strong features and a warm smile. Every hair on his head was perfectly cut into a flat top and he wore a neatly trimmed full beard. His eyes were a soft golden brown. He wasn't a big man, maybe 5'9" and 140 pounds, but he seemed strong, very strong.

Over the next four days there were lots of opportunities to see Oscar interacting with the staff of this ship. It turned out that not only the officers worked for Oscar but so did everyone on the ship. He was actually just visiting the ship; he worked in Miami as Vice President of Operations for the cruise line and all the crew on two ships worked for him. It didn't matter if it was an officer or a room steward, he gave each of them his thoughtful attention. I could see the respect and fondness all of the crew had for him. That told me so much about this caring and smart man. I was definitely falling in love with him. He was honorable and I could see he was reliable. He was well-read. We had great conversations and very comfortable silences.

He was also eighteen years older than me and had six children. He told me during those four days that he was also still legally married. My heart plunged. He said that ten years earlier he and his wife had lost a child, a baby girl who died when she was only a few days old. They'd had two children after that in an effort to save their marriage, but it failed. Essentially, he told me, they had lived separate lives for the last ten years.

When we said our goodbyes, we both expressed hope that our encounter was just a beginning. I went home to Dallas changed.

Over the next few weeks, we spoke every day, long lingering phone conversations. He was going to come visit only two weeks later and I couldn't wait. That weekend we declared our love, and I also asked him to go back to his wife and make sure in his heart and hers that there wasn't any unfinished business. One week later he said it was done. Anyone I talked to said I was insane. He was eighteen years older than me and a sailor. He probably had a girl in every port. But I was thinking about the future, not the past. It was only six weeks from the day we met until we were engaged. Now to tell his children.

I knew I just met my destiny, but he lived in Florida and I lived in Dallas. My children lived in Dallas. I wanted to stay close to my children, but I also felt out of place in the life my ex and his new wife were building. The children were in private schools, lived in a dream home, and seemed happy. Although I hated leaving the city where my children were, I had to follow the calling of a life with Oscar. The future was bright.

Getting to the Chapel

Every day I'd hurry home from work, waiting for the phone to ring. There were no cell phones in those days. Oscar and I talked on the phone every day, revisiting all our dreams. His voice comforted me and made me smile. We didn't talk about politics; we talked about what we did that day. We talked about history, places we'd seen in our lives, and about faith. I was comforted to know that we both wanted God to be part of our lives. I never wanted to hang up the phone. What stands out most about those calls is the listening that went on. We were both sharing, talking and actively listening. We told each other the stories of our lives. Imagine how many hours we spent on the phone in order to get to know each other well enough to get engaged only six weeks after we met. Perhaps long-distance courtship was a prelude to Internet dating, which would become popular decades later.

I told Oscar about my polio and my dad's battle with cancer and my lonely childhood and my arranged marriage. I told him about my ex-husband and my time in the cult. "I don't want to be surprised by secrets," I explained. "I'd rather know up front everything I need to know about you."

I continued, "I've lived much of my life in silence and I want to know that what I think and how I feel will be heard and will matter." I confessed that I had a lot of emotional scars from losing my children and a lot of trust issues—but, I assured him, the scars were not who I was.

"I don't have a dream about a particular china pattern or certain kind of house I want," I said. "I don't care about what kind of car I drive, as long as it is dependable and clean and has not a single bumper sticker."

We laughed and laughed. We both wanted a second chance at love and honesty in marriage; a second chance to have wonderful relationships with the eight children we had between us. We agreed we did not want to have more children. Because this was a mature adult second relationship, we knew we needed more than just the passion that existed between us. We needed to discuss faith and money and goals and dreams, which would guide our path toward a successful marriage.

I learned that Oscar grew up in the shadow of a Detroit car plant, where his working-class family dreamed of sending him to work one day. His father had immigrated from Belgium at the age of 12. As a first-generation immigrant, Pa cherished the opportunity to work toward the American dream, which for him was at the Chrysler car plant; however, that was never Oscar's dream.

"I started working when I was just a boy, pulling a wagon around the neighborhood, selling fruits and vegetables," Oscar told me with pride in his voice. "I helped the milkman deliver the glass jars to porches, and summers I worked on my uncle's dairy farm."

Oscar told me that he was the oldest of three. He had a sister five years younger and a brother who was 10 years younger. "My Ma and Pa always expected me to keep an eye out for my little sister." Ma was definitely a strong personality whose presence commanded respect. With ten years between Oscar and his little brother, Herbie, they didn't get a lot of time together. By the time Herbie was born Oscar was ten and already working.

I got the impression that his family lived in the middle of the union battles that surrounded the Detroit car plants and while Pa was a man of small stature, he could hold his own. It didn't seem at all strange to hear some of the stories, as I remember hearing my mother also tell stories that during her childhood in Chicago, Al Capone was a neighbor at one time. There was a rough and tumble side to Oscar and somewhere around the age of 12 he got into a little trouble. The judge told him he could either go to juvenile detention or seminary school. He got on the train for San Antonio and looked forward to seminary school. He spent 9 months there and for a time thought perhaps he should become a priest. He loves telling people that he went to seminary and studied to become a priest. I always tilt my head and add, "That was only because the judge gave him the option."

When he got home, however, girls got in the way of that plan. He was distracted in school and wanted to do better. He told his Pa, "I want to go to St. Joseph's," a private all boys' school. When Pa said the family could not afford that, Oscar got a job so that he could pay his own high school tuition. He worked at a printing shop, where he was valuable as a tiny guy who could get in places the other men could not. "I was paid in cash under the table, because it was illegal for me to be working at that age," Oscar explained. He treasured his time at the Christian Brothers' school and did well for the most part.

In his last year of high school, he told his Pa, "I want to go to college."

"College is not for our kind," Pa told him. "Our kind works in the factories."

Oscar knew he was not going to work in the factories, so one year later, when he was the first in his family to graduate high school, he joined the Navy. He had to have his parents' permission at the time. His mother's brothers had been Marines, but she would not give permission for the Marines. In her mind, the Navy was safer.

My parents always told me it didn't matter what we did for a living as long as we worked hard and gave a good day's work for a good day's pay. I knew by the story of Oscar's early life that he adhered to this same principle. *My dad would be happy with this man's work ethic, I thought. I respect this man.*

He spent six years in the Navy, during which time he got married and started having children. When he got out of the Navy, he couldn't find a suitable job. The Coast Guard recruiter said they could take him in at the same rank he was in the Navy. He saw those Coast Guard ships always in port and he thought he would like a duty station that kept him close to home and his wife and children, so he joined, finding out only afterward that the Coast Guard ships did not stay in port. He served on ice breakers and battleships far from home for long periods of time.

He and his wife had three children by then with a fourth on the way. He was away at sea when he got the news that his baby girl had been born. A few days later he was summoned to the Captain's office to hear the news that his baby daughter had died. He needed to get home and take care of his family, but confessed to the Captain that he didn't have enough money even to bury his daughter. The captain promised him help through the Coast Guard Welfare Fund, established for just this kind of situation. Oscar was grateful and humbled.

They really weren't happy during their 28-year marriage. They played in a bowling league, attended church and family gatherings on Sundays. Delores was a stay-at-home mom, like most mothers in those days. I got the impression that Oscar always felt last on her list. The death of their baby began the end of their marriage. It is said some marriages never survive the loss of a child. They remained married and had more children, but the fragile bond between them was never the same.

A few years after Oscar went into the Coast Guard, he decided he needed to advance so he could get more money for his grow-ing family. He went to his wife and declared he was going to take the path to becoming an officer. She laughed at him, which only made him all the more determined. He was nearing the cut-off age to qualify for officer's candidate school. He was finally accepted with no time to spare, just shortly after his 33rd birthday. Boot camp, as the oldest trainee, wasn't easy, but he applied himself with a strength brought about by determination, grit and neces-sity. During officer's candidate school his father-in-law died and some would say he wasn't caring because he didn't leave school to attend the funeral; however, if he left, he would have had to start all over again upon return. He couldn't do that. He knew his father-in-law would understand. Then he hurt his leg, but he con-tinued on, doing his morning runs on crutches. This man would not be deterred. He graduated and became an officer, moving up the ranks until he retired as a Lieutenant Commander with 25 years of service.

As I listened to Oscar's life story it made me see that he was willing to be open and vulnerable. He was willing to show me his scars. In such a short time I already had very strong feelings for Oscar. We had a magnetic connection—I was so drawn to him.

He told me two important things about his first marriage that would be different if he were to marry me. First, he wanted to know that his well-being would be considered, not just the well-being of the children. *I can do that and I so appreciate him being clear and upfront about this need.* Second, Oscar told me his first wife had spent every nickel he ever made and then some. He made it clear that he wanted to live debt-free and he would never give me all of his money. *I love that we are voicing our needs out loud. This is so much more than passion. I care deeply about this man and he has convinced me that he cares for me.*

I met Oscar six years after his retirement from the military and at the time he was in his glory days as VP of a cruise line. Through storytelling and sharing, I learned about the very core and foundation that gave this man the strength I saw in him. He was strong to go against the storms of disbelief and forge his own destiny. He had an inner compass that kept him facing toward the north and moving forward toward his dreams. He was humble and kind when he listened and helped those that worked for him. He always had an ear. I was smitten and in love. *I can trust my heart with this man. I can see him and he sees me for myself.*

Each time we'd talk on the phone Oscar expressed how grateful he was for the attention that I paid him. How could I not? I was so curious and infatuated with this man. At 48 years old, he was easy to the eyes. He was strong for a medium-built man, with strong legs built by years of standing watch on the open sea. This man I met could plant himself in a position and there was no tossing him about.

I had just spent six years in a life of wild craziness with no direction or anchor. Oscar's strength and steadiness and his inner compass were comforting and appealing to me. He made me feel secure, loved and hopeful. He was also playful and adventurous. He wanted to give me the world. He told me over and over again that I was his world. He was a perfect officer and gentleman. He opened doors and pulled out chairs. He glowed when he introduced me to anyone. How could I not fall in love with this attentive, adoring, strong, determined man?

He also shared personal things with me that let me in to his fears and guilts and a darker side. *He isn't perfect, and I am so glad because neither am I. I can be myself with him. We both see each other— really see each other.*

The early months of getting to know each other felt like finding our way out of a deep fog, following a mariner's compass that was guiding and navigating us to each other. We each needed personal attention and acceptance, despite our pasts or because of them. We sensed, as we spent hours talking on the phone and visiting, that the points on that compass could lead us to a fairy-tale life filled with magic. Of course, fairy tales also have dragons and demons, but together we could slay them and overcome. We had both travelled a very long way in our personal journeys. Together, we sensed, we just might be unstoppable. *He's looking at me, really looking at me,* I thought, *and I'm so surprised that that makes me feel safe and comfortable.*

Shortly before we were married there was a maritime convention being held in New York City. Oscar asked me if I wanted to go. "Ah—yeah!" I replied enthusiastically. He said we'd have a little time to explore the city and then there would be a gala for us to attend. *What do I wear to a gala?* I wondered. Oscar said he would make the flight arrangements and he was sending me some shopping money to buy my gala attire. He'd be wearing a tuxedo. *Wow. I just have to remember to stand straight, good posture and have good manners. I hear you, Mother, "always watch your manners."* He was going to introduce me to everyone he knew in the marine industry.

Neiman Marcus at NorthPark in Dallas was my favorite place to shop for clothes. Usually, I could only afford to buy something there on their annual sale day. While Oscar had given me a generous sum, I had to buy not only a dress but also shoes, an evening bag and jewelry. I found my way to a second-hand consignment store and found a beautiful white full-length evening gown. It was sleeveless with a scoop neck and an empire top, which was entirely beaded. Layers of flowing white chiffon went from the beading to the floor. It fit like a glove. *Gloves. I need gloves.* I bought the dress and went to Neiman Marcus to look for gloves. I found the most beautiful translucent white gloves embellished with a flower at the wrist. Then I found beaded pumps. I was ready for the gala.

I flew to New York and Oscar was anxiously waiting for me when I got off the plane. He had a meeting that afternoon, but he got me settled in at the hotel. I asked if we were going to get to see a musical. "I don't think we can get tickets for tonight," he said. It was our only free night, but he said I could try. As soon as he left for his meeting, I scurried down to the concierge desk. Acting like I knew what I was doing, I said, "I want good seats for a musical tonight." The concierge made some calls and found seats in about row J to see *Me and My Gal.* Perfect.

I don't remember dinner or anything else about that day. We were going to a Broadway musical! Hooray! We cleaned up and off we went. The theatre was beautiful and there was a buzz of excitement as the patrons waited with eager anticipation. The next thing I remember is a singer standing in the aisle right next to our chairs looking at us while he was singing, startling us awake. Yes—we were so tired, we had fallen asleep. How embarrassing. The first of many times I wished I were invisible. Oh well. I still don't feel like I really have seen a Broadway musical.

The next day we went to a New York deli, where the tables were tiny and crowded together for optimum seating. I looked at the menu and just could not decide.

"Order whatever you want, darling," Oscar said.

"Really?" When the waitress came, I told her I wanted a bagel with lox and cream cheese, a bowl of matzo ball soup, potato pancakes with applesauce on the side and an order of matzo brie.

"Miss, each of those items is an entrée in itself. Are you sure you want all of that?"

"Yes ma'am. I want to taste everything." She shook her head as she left the table. They had to bring a little side table over because there wasn't enough room for everything I ordered. *My mother would not be happy with me right now.* Her dating advice had been to never order the most expensive thing on the menu and always leave something on your plate, otherwise, the gentleman might think you'd be too high maintenance.

But Oscar didn't care. He was so excited and tickled to see me joyfully trying all these favorite foods here at the famous New York deli. *This food is so delicious. I will never be hungry again. This strong handsome man is stable. I'm on top of the world.*

We walked a little after our meal and did some Fifth Avenue window-shopping. I admired a grey wool dress with grey suede knee high boots. Oscar told me to try them on.

"No, I couldn't." The weekend had already cost a fortune.

"Try them on," he encouraged.

The dress looked marvelous. It had a mock turtleneck with long sleeves and fit every curve. I was a petite little thing—maybe a size 2 or 4 and every curve had the right proportion...35-24-35. The dress looked marvelous, especially with those boots. We left the store with packages in hand. I was so excited and Oscar was delighted to shower me with gifts. I wore the heck out of that dress for the next decade. The extravagant purchase was a great value in the end.

Now it was time to take a breath and get ready for the gala. I took my time with my makeup and hair. Oscar could tie a perfect bowtie for his tuxedo. He looked so dapper. I stepped out of the bathroom and asked him to zip me up. He was working on it and then I heard him whisper, "shit." I hadn't heard him cuss before.

"What happened?" He was struggling with the zipper and it broke. OMG. We need to go downstairs for the gala in five minutes!

Being always prepared, as he is, he dug in his bag and came out with a safety pin. He messed around back there for ten minutes but finally got something rigged, so I'd be able to wear my dress to the ball. I put on the gloves and my jewelry and the wonderful beaded shoes. I tucked my evening bag under my arm and slipped my arm through his while he led me down to the great double doors to enter the gala. I felt like every eye was on me as we made our grand entrance. He was so proud. I was so scared. *Oh Lord please don't let that zipper pop.*

The ballroom was huge, with tables 3 or 4 deep circling a large dance floor. A live band was playing. *We'll be dancing tonight.* We found our way to the assigned seating and made our introductions and got comfortable. It was a lovely night. My zipper stayed intact. My warning to all the ladies would be about beaded shoes. With every step I took I had to give a little tug on the chiffon that was catching on those dang beaded shoes. Nevertheless, it was an enchanting evening indeed, filled with dancing, good food and friendly conversation. *Oh my gosh, I feel loved. I am in love with this man.*

It was time to introduce Oscar to my children. I just knew they would also fall in love with him. *Lord, please help them all to love each other.* He was experienced with children, having six of his own. Oddly enough, his youngest child was only three years older than my oldest child, making them all stair-stepped, which was remarkable given the eighteen years between Oscar and myself. They seemed star-struck when they met him, like he was larger than life. He told them a little bit about his adventures sailing around the world and through the ice and playing with penguins. He expressed interest in their activities and asked them what they liked. My daughter, at eleven years old, thought he looked just like Kenny Rogers. She fell in love instantly. They both liked him. What was not to like? I asked my son if it was OK if I married Oscar. He wanted to know if Oscar was a Christian. At 9 years old, my son knew he wanted me to marry a man of faith. Well—I had found my Prince Charming who looked like Kenny Rogers and was a man of strong faith. My children gave me their permission to marry Oscar. They were in fact thrilled for me. Maybe they didn't really realize that it would mean I'd be moving. We just all knew how great we felt when the four of us were together.

Six weeks after we met, during one of our long telephone conversations, Oscar declared that he didn't want to live without me and asked very simply if I would marry him.

"Yes, I will marry you." *He fills my every thought.*

Playing on the radio at the time were songs like Paul Young's "Every time you go away, you take a piece of me with you," and that described it exactly. Lionel Richie was singing "Stuck on You," describing the feeling deep in our souls. Then there was Foreigner who said it best in their song "I Want to Know What Love Is," adding, "in my life there's been heartache and pain and I just want to go where love is." I would cry when I heard these songs because they said so perfectly what my heart was feeling.

He wanted to buy me an engagement ring. I said I had a one-carat diamond solitaire that my mother had given me from her ring when my father died and I would always want to wear it. We decided to buy a guard to circle the solitaire to be my wedding ring, but we would get something different as my engagement ring. We found a lovely ring with an oval ruby in the center circled by 10 diamonds. I have received such pleasure from that ruby ring and over the years we added to my collection of rubies, with earrings, a necklace and a diamond and ruby bracelet.

Eleven months after we met, Oscar and I got married. We decided to have a simple wedding in Dallas, renting a chapel by the hour, which included the minster, the music and the flowers. My mother and sister flew in from California, and Oscar's oldest son flew in to be the best man. My best friend Kathy was my maid of honor and my children were our wedding party.

It was time. My mother and sister asked me the standard last-minute question, "Are you sure you want to do this?" My mind was racing with all the things in my life that were about to change as my mother helped me step into my wedding dress. I was so glad my mother was there. I wore my Sweet Sixteen dress for my first wedding and though tradition says you only wear white for your first wedding, I wore a pure white wedding dress this time around. It had ruffles at the shoulders and all around the edge of the full-length train. I wore a hat instead of a veil. Oscar and I had nothing to hide.

Wedding day

The photographer was in the dressing room with us, capturing the mother and daughter precious moments, when the wedding coordinator came in to the bride's dressing area and said it was time to go down the aisle. My mother took one look at me and said, "she isn't ready." Tapping her finger on her watch, the coordinator reminded us we were paying by the hour. My mother said, "I'll pay for the extra time." I was excited, but scared to death and I didn't want to be rushed.

I'm sure there were gasps when the chapel doors opened. My dear friend Don Allen, who had kept a watchful eye out for me during my single years, had taken the time to get to know Oscar. He was glad to walk me down the aisle and give me away to a man he had come to admire. Satisfaction, joy and excitement filled me up when I saw Oscar with his son and mine beside him. My best friend Kathy was also waiting for me, standing beside my daughter, who was glowing. I knew I was doing the right thing to marry this man that stood before me.

We recited the standard vows to each other, to have and to hold from that day forward, for better, for worse, for richer, for poorer, in sickness and in health, to love and to cherish for the rest of our lives. We each said I do. We looked forward to proving the naysayers wrong. Ha—some thought it wouldn't last. We had a lot of odds against us. We had a full generation of eighteen years that separated us, but our love and respect and desire for the well-being of each other was as strong as the ocean that had brought us together.

We celebrated with a small reception at a Chinese restaurant in a private room. Our small guest list was quite continental. Besides my mom, sister and Oscar's son who flew in, one of Oscar's close friends flew in from New York. Oscar's beloved Uncle Bud and Aunt Joann drove up from Houston to attend. None of the other family or friends from Oscar's life were there, because we were planning a big second reception for the Florida family and friends. It didn't seem odd at all that we invited my ex-husband and his new wife to join us. They were after all part of my life, as we shared the children. I wanted them to have every opportunity to

Just married!

see Oscar so they would trust him for a life of upcoming long distance visitations. My dear Big Daddy, Tom James, came with his wife, Bobbie. Everyone wanted to see me marry this sailor guy. They were a little bit concerned because of the age difference, but everyone could see just how in love we were, and their blessings enveloped us. It was pure joy, as our happiness was clear and it was evident that this was something exceptionally good.

However, it was time to face the music. I would not see all of these friends and family again for some time. I was leaving Texas and the easy access to my children. I told Oscar there must always be enough money for plane tickets. He had no problem with that. He intended to give me the world.

Blending Family

Back on that momentous day when we met, in June 1984, it was the beginning of a life full of endless possibilities. Three months before we were married, I decided I should go ahead and move to Florida to be with Oscar. When he told me he was living in his travel trailer, I pictured something quite romantic. But when we pulled up, I let out a big sigh. This 24' foot travel trailer sure didn't look romantic. I was sitting in the car in a new city waiting to go inside. *OK Adrienne you can do this.* Less than 300 square feet isn't much space, but inside it was cozy and clean. Oscar reassured me, telling me that the next day I could start looking for a rental home or apartment. "This way you can choose what's comfortable for you." *That's a relief. Now this might be like an adventure.*

You find out things about someone once you live together. I was hoping for no big surprises this time around. It was a roller coaster of feelings. I was missing my children and my friend Kathy so very much, but I was happy to be with Oscar.

One morning I called Kathy crying. "What have I done?"

"It'll be OK," she said, as always. She is the best cheerleader and friend a girl could hope to know.

It did feel somewhat comfortable to be in Florida again. I loved living by the ocean. I surprised myself by how much trust I immediately had for Oscar. Truthfully, I doubted myself and my own judgment the most. This was crazy. However, I was committed and excited. I felt like now I had the chance to find out who I wanted to be.

I was getting ready to walk into an entirely new world, meeting Oscar's friends, co-workers, parents and children. *I want to be myself. Will they like me? I need to put my best foot forward.* My dear friend Tom reminded me again, "The biggest gift you can give him is to make his children love you." That would be a tall order, since I wasn't sure if I loved myself.

"Adrienne, you take yourself wherever you go," my mother would say. I wanted to bring the best of myself to this new life, and leave the bad behind. I felt excited. I felt intimidated. It was daunting to step into this new world.

He took me first to meet his parents. He already told me a lot about them. I knew they were working-class folks. Ma was a short, stout woman with a warm embrace. She was cooking home-made applesauce with cinnamon candies for spice, and the house smelled delicious. Pa, who worked in the Chrysler plant in Detroit his whole life, walking the same steps from his house to his shop every day of his career, was recently retired. They were open and kind, asking a lot of questions. Ma first wanted to know if we were planning on having children. I said, "No—my two and his six are plenty enough."

Next, she asked, "How do you think it will be to have sex with a man 18 years older than you?" I was shocked. My family didn't speak of such things. The only sex talk I had had with my reserved mother was the night before my arranged marriage, when she told me not to be afraid. I quickly found out that my future mother-in-law was not going to be shy at all. I told her I wasn't worried about it and quickly changed the subject. I think they were shocked at just how young I was, but they made an effort to welcome me in.

Now it was time to meet his children. It would take a while for them to warm up to me. Since they were a military family, he told them before we met, it was OK if they didn't like me, but they must treat me with respect. I really wanted them to like me. His oldest, a son, was 4 years younger than me and we met at the wedding because he was Oscar's best man. Oscar's oldest daughter already had 3 children of her own so when I married into the family, I was an instant grandmother at only 31 years old.

We all made the effort to get to know each other and like each other. The house we rented had a pool in the backyard. The best memories of my childhood had been around a swimming pool. The waters carried strong healing powers for body and soul. His children would come over and spend time swimming and Oscar would grill hamburgers and hotdogs and pork chops. It set the stage for an atmosphere of relaxation and fun. There was storytelling as we all lounged poolside. They asked me a lot of questions about my childhood and my children. I asked them about their hobbies and dreams. The youngest was dreaming of being a veterinarian. Another daughter wanted to be a cartoonist for Disney. When they left for the day, there were hugs and talk of the next visit. His children could see that he was happier than ever. While it was hard for them to see their parents get divorced, they recognized that it should have happened years earlier. We all wanted this to work.

Oscar's second oldest daughter was an ally. She would encourage the younger girls to give me a chance. I liked the girls. One was sweet and one was feisty. They had good table manners. They seemed to speak their minds, and despite my not being much older than them, if I asked a question that called for a simple yes or no answer, they always said, "yes ma'am" or "no ma'am." I lived in Texas so I knew about "ma'am," but I didn't realize that addressing someone with "sir" or "ma'am" was also the military way. This was pretty amazing because they were teenage girls when we met—the two youngest were ages 14 and 16. I can't imagine how hard it was for them. We only lived about 10 miles from Oscar's first wife, Delores. We tried to never speak ill of each other's ex-spouses to any of the children. We were respectful of the fact that Oscar had been married to her for 28 years and she was the mother of his children and raised them mostly on her own while he was at sea. She deserved respect. While obviously there were irreconcilable differences or they would not have divorced, that was not an open discussion with the children. I never felt like I broke up the marriage. Oscar always told me that it was already broken. Even the children assured me that I was not the cause of the divorce, but I'm sure there were moments of doubt. I told the girls I just hoped we would be friends.

Call it fate or destiny, but my oldest step-daughter and I shared an unusual circumstance. She also was a mother without custody. She had two daughters in her first marriage and a son with her current husband. For a period of time, the daughters lived with their dad. Neither she nor I knew of any other women walking that journey and so even without words we formed a connection immediately. We had our issues, but we also shared an unbelievable grief which was a deep bond. She lived hours away in a different city from her girls. I lived a plane ride away from my children. We both knew how it felt to be the mom *not* tucking in our children at night. It was perfect for her to use our home to have her visitations with the girls. It wasn't always easy, but it was a good way for us to get to know each other, even Oscar. He didn't always have the best relationship with his children when they were young. At sea much of their childhood, when he was home, he ran a tight ship. From the stories I've heard, the children were encouraged by their mother to keep their distance from him, saying, "He'll be gone soon enough."

Now, we started blending the families. New starts and new beginnings held new possibilities. It seemed like a good start. My children would come and visit and we were all getting to know each other. My mother, who thought nothing of moving from one coast to another, relocated again, moving cross-country to Florida to be near us and be part of the blending process.

On one of our first Christmas holidays together, I wanted to do something special for the girls. That morning as each daughter arrived and stepped in through the sliding glass door, they were shocked, asking, "Who is that?"

I smiled and replied, "He's your Christmas present."

A handsome young man stood in a tuxedo bowtie with a big smile on his face.

"You have the day off," I explained. "I hired this handsome young man to be my helper for the day."

I wanted them to just be able to enjoy their day without chores: no setting tables or serving and definitely no dishes to do.

Oscar was living his dream, working for the cruise line and also working part-time as a ship surveyor with his mentor and dear friend, Captain Hofstra. I landed a great job. We were at the top of our game, able to shower the blended family with gifts and begin living out our dreams.

It did get messy sometimes. There were times we'd put everything in the blender—kids, grandkids, feelings, expectations, past hurts and hopes—and hit the "on" switch, only to realize that we'd left the lid off. Oscar had only been retired from the military six years when I met him. His kids still knew that strict military dad. They were getting to know a different man now, a little more relaxed. Dad's not in the military anymore; he's divorced; and he has married this young woman. Every one of those changes was major. They were teenagers and as teenagers do, they pushed the envelope a little. We had family events where we had to be together with his ex-wife. There were proms and teenage weddings—oh my. Without any discussion about it, the adults knew we needed to be civil to each other, at the very least for these events. The kids were making the effort to spend time with us and to get comfortable with this new situation, but it was understandable that they would maintain a certain protectiveness for their mom.

One of the girls married her high school sweetheart. Daddy walked her down the aisle and we hoped for the best. What more can you do? It didn't work out so well, so we helped her get a divorce a short time later. The details are her story, not mine, but it was messy. They never wanted to introduce their guys to Dad, at least not the dad of their younger years. He had the reputation of meeting the boys at the front door with his gun in its holster hanging off his shoulder. Breaking through those established barriers and walls was my job, as I saw it. We needed to demolish the old rules of relationship and begin remodeling the structure for our future with this family.

Just Around the Corner

My heart holds a willingness to take risks, not so much with money, but with other things. Perhaps that's a trait I inherited from my dad, who held on to his dreams and the endless possibilities always just around the corner. I know I have his hazel eyes and his high cheekbones. I recognize him when I look in the mirror and it comforts me to know that he lives on in me. I am more like my dad than just the physical features, because Dad was a dreamer and wanted adventure. When Oscar and I talked about travel and exploration, it felt familiar and comfortable. There was a spark inside of me at the thought of every part of it. Sure, I wanted to see other places, but it also served as a good way for Oscar and me to get to know each other better and to spend time with family and friends. We began to weave our passion for travel together with our desire to be close to our loved ones. It's important to me to make the effort to maintain and build strong sincere relationships. Since our family and friends were scattered everywhere, travel would be a good way to coordinate uninterrupted time. I thought to myself, *I hope that the special moments we share can make up for all the moments we miss.*

As a child, travel had been introduced to me early when I was growing up in southern California. When I was only eight or nine, we made several visits to Vegas. Mom and I would spend all day poolside with her Bain de Soleil SPF 4, while Dad and my brother Mickey played golf. In the evening we'd go to a lavish buffet dinner and see a Vegas show full of music and sparkly showgirls.

A few years later, right after my dad was diagnosed with cancer, he decided to fulfill a dream and bought a VW camper van. It was a brand-new model with a pop-up roof, perfect for weekend camping trips. That was my first introduction to camping. One time Dad found a new resort-style campground near San Diego with a pool and clubhouse. It was way out in the boondocks, so there were only a few campers there. We swam and ate and shot pool and I thought it was wonderful family time. We didn't keep that camper, though. I don't think Mom thought it was so much fun. Those experiences planted a seed in me that I wouldn't know was still alive and growing for years. Travel would be become the first of many passions in my life.

When I was fifteen, a year after dad's cancer diagnosis, it was a miracle that he was still surviving. Needing a break from the reality of cancer, my folks decided to take a cruise, while Dad was still able to travel. That was the first time I heard about cruising; I knew someday I'd get to go on a cruise. They decided to leave me behind, alone, asking the neighbors to look in on me. I was fine home alone for the most part. I do remember breaking the rules and having a boy come to the condo. Nothing happened, but I broke the rules. Also, I didn't have my driver's license yet, but I had keys to the car and I'd been practicing with my dad. I took the car out for a spin. If any of the neighbors saw these things, they didn't tell my folks. Perhaps my folks hadn't really asked anyone to look in on me after all? I didn't like breaking the rules. It wasn't really fun. Looking back, I am so glad my parents did that cruise while they could. It's exactly what I hear now, as my friends get older or lose a spouse: "do it while you can," a lesson I saw in action early on.

Some girls dream of their wedding day or the home they'll live in, but I dreamed about vacations. It seemed natural to me to want to go on a cruise, when my boss gave me a vacation for my 30th birthday. On the top deck of the ship, under the stars that first night we talked, Oscar told me his dream was to travel. He loved the sea, of course, but he also wanted to see the USA. He wanted to go camping and cruising. Travel sounded romantic and adventurous to me. My heart raced with excitement. I was ready to see the world with Oscar, who had already seen much of it. This lonely, shy girl was about to be bold and adventurous and have the time of her life.

Our first married adventure was our honeymoon. Oscar knew Ted Arison, founder of Carnival Cruise lines, because they were all in the industry together. We received tickets to cruise aboard the *Mardi Gras*. The day after our wedding we flew from Dallas to Miami, boarded the ship and found complimentary tour passes waiting in our cabin. The second night we were invited to dine at the captain's table. They seated me right next to the captain. Oh dear. My mother would say, "If you have manners, you can go anywhere." I was so glad manners were instilled in me. We went to Cozumel, Grand Cayman and Ocho Rios, Jamaica. Our tour in Ocho Rios took us on a 600' climb up Dunn's River Falls. The steep incline and slippery rocks were the hardest physical challenge of my life. Oscar was leading and pulling me and some strange man was behind me with his hand on my butt pushing. *I did it. I made it to the top. Am I dreaming?*

For my children's first visit after my marriage, they took their first unaccompanied minor flight at ages 10 and 12 and we took them on a cruise so they could see firsthand what Oscar did. We gave them the tour of the *Emerald Seas*, the ship where Oscar and I met. The kids were itching to get off on their own. While the ship was safe for them to wander off, I made sure to remind them that every worker on that ship worked for Oscar, so all eyes would be on them. We had to figure out what they were going to call Oscar. They already had a dad, so it didn't seem right for them to call him Dad. Oscar's girls called him Daddy. It didn't take long to settle on Pops, and so began a deep and loving adoration going both ways between Pops and Leah and Nathan.

All too soon our time together was over and they headed back to Dallas. The farewells were heart-wrenching. I sobbed for days. I prayed that someday they would know my heart and that this situation and separation would not be forever. *Please God keep our hearts together.* No sooner did they leave than I got busy planning their next visit. It always seemed too far off. We wrote letters to each other and talked on the phone.

Traveling enlarged my life. The adventure of it all was exciting, but I realize now that the time spent planning was a good distraction. Focusing on all the details required to coordinate and find the perfect spot with the exact right activities was part of the experience. By the age of 31, I had already experienced physical, mental, emotional, spiritual and financial adversity. I learned to cope and overcome. I didn't consciously set out to acquire these skills—it was instinct. This new enthusiasm and curiosity that filled me up also attracted people and light into my extraordinary new life. My legs felt strong. I could dance and hike. I was having a blast. It was fun and exciting to travel and meet new people. I felt like a princess who had been rescued by my prince and taken to a land where fairy tales come true. I still struggled on the inside with my demons and old voices, but I could quiet them a little more easily. I was still finding my way spiritually and had a lot to contemplate, but I had hope again. As I got to know Oscar and my love and trust grew, I was grateful and optimistic. Life was looking up.

There were more relationships to build. Now that I could afford to travel, I began to want to get reacquainted with my brothers and sister. My sister married and moved away when I was only nine. My oldest brother moved away shortly thereafter. My folks and I moved out of state when I was thirteen, and then I had virtually no contact with my siblings while I was in the commune. During my single years, I only saw them a few times because I didn't have the money. I wanted to get to know them as adults. Only a short time after we were married, Oscar arranged for all four of us and our spouses to cruise on one of his ships, the *Azure Seas*, sailing from California. The entire crew worked for Oscar and they paid close attention to his family. That week was my first introduction to Senor Frogs. The eight of us did the conga, drank and ate and were darn right silly. Thank goodness we made it back to the ship. We had such fun together and it confirmed we all really liked each other. *Thank you, God—I see a future entwined with my family.*

We began to explore the world of camping/RVing, deciding to go to northern Florida on an RV trip. In St. Augustine, Oscar set up a nice campsite. I settled the inside of the trailer, pulling everything out that had been stored away for riding down the highway. The next day, hand in hand, we explored historic St. Augustine. We were settled down for the night when all of a sudden there was a pounding on the door. It was the sheriff.

"Are you Mr. Poppe?"

"Yes sir."

"Your office needs you to call them right away."

"What the heck? How did they find us? What is going on?"

Oscar went to the payphone and called his secretary. When he returned, he said, "We have to leave ASAP."

His secretary knew we were going to the St. Augustine area, but didn't know where exactly. She had the sheriff's department checking every campground in the area to find us.

Oscar told me anxiously, "They need me back in Miami. There's been a fire aboard the *Emerald Seas*. They've evacuated the passengers and they want me there before the Coast Guard comes on board in the morning for the investigation."

It was a wild drive back. Seventeen passengers were treated, but they were OK. The fire was contained. Thank goodness.

It may have been that incident when I learned more about the gender of ships. Most importantly, a ship is a *she*, not an *it*. Also, it's not a boat, it's a ship. When we talked about a ship or went aboard a ship, Oscar talked with such affection about her. His eyes were on every inch of her. It was then I started telling people, "When we visit a ship, we visit one of Oscar's girlfriends." Ships ranked first, then the dogs, then me. Well, not really but he certainly loved his ships. It didn't bother me. Ah—the sea, the salt, the power of the waves and those ships. They were his passion... so many ships and so many adventures.

As we continued to build relationships and explore the United States, this one time we flew and met my sister and her husband in Santa Fe, then drove the High Road to Taos to tour the pueblo. It was our stop along the way at Chimayo that touched me deeply.

We visited a chapel carved into the mountain like a cave, with a dirt floor and a small inner sanctuary. The spirit there is powerful, filled with the prayers of all those who have walked miles and miles for many years to bring their prayer requests to the healing energy of the earth that is there. I was overcome by emotion and cried. Words can be so inadequate. I felt that I waited my whole life to get to this room where no words were necessary. The silent prayers of my heart moved in a swaying rhythm within my body and that was how I prayed. The art, the earth, the pueblos and Chimayo brought stillness to my soul. I fell in love with New Mexico and I knew God was listening.

Sometimes the object of a trip would be to explore a great place. Sometimes an event or festival would call us. When we weren't travelling, we spent a lot of time talking about travelling and dreaming about the next adventure. While some of our trips were necessary because of work or family visits, they were reflective of our growing passion for the art of travel. We loved it and we were getting pretty good at it too!

One of my favorite places to visit was Little Stirrup Cay in the Bahamas, the private island used by the cruise lines as a port stop. Oscar brought a group of men together to develop that island and one of the guys was Ray, an old shipmate of Oscar's who served deep on the rivers in Vietnam. Ray was not afraid of anything. The story goes that the island was raw and an easy target for aerial drug drops. Oscar had Ray and his band of brothers rid the island of the drug lords, clean it up and bring in utilities. Just like that it became a destination beach stop for the cruise lines. I wasn't afraid of the ocean so we would swim way out and chase the waves. The sun was a perfect temperature and so were the frozen drinks, wearing us out in such a good way. We left enough time for an afternoon nap before getting ready for dinner on the ship, often at the captain's table.

We were friends now with Captain Michael, the most handsome Greek man I've ever seen. He was married to Mari, a beautiful and sweet English girl with fair skin and silky hair. She was well mannered and funny. The officers mingled at night with the passengers and there was dancing and partying in the ship disco until the wee hours of the night. Oscar and I could cut a pretty good rug and we liked to dance. *Thank you, God, that Oscar likes to dance. OMG. We are having so much fun.* This path we were on was raining blessings and filled with sunshine and light.

Captain Michael's wife, Mari, was aboard on the first time I sailed through the Panama Canal. During the day Oscar would work and I would sunbathe or take a tour on my own. Whatever I wanted was mine for the asking. I respected that privilege and did not abuse it. One evening Mari asked me if I wanted to join her the next day for shopping. As the captain's wife, she knew exactly where we should go and what shops had reliable merchandise. The next day we got off the ship in Cartagena, Colombia. Disembarkation can be chaos no matter what port the ship is visiting. Passengers get assigned a number and wait for their turn to leave the ship. I was with Mari so we didn't need a number. At the bottom of the gangway passengers are met by taxi cabs and locals shouting and clamoring for the passengers who need a tour or a trinket. It's a mess of activity. Your eyes need to scan quickly while not making eye contact with any of the hawkers, until you see your tour guide holding a paddle high with the name of the tour. This time I just kept my eyes on Mari, since Captain Michael had a taxi waiting for us. It whisked us away to the center of town to a jewelry shop Mari knew about. Columbia is known as the best place to buy emeralds. *OMG. Pinch me. I'm in Cartagena, Colombia spending the day with the captain's wife.*

The counters were filled with all types of beautiful jewelry. Although we were living in the fast lane now, our budget was in the far right slow lane. We still had all those unaccompanied minor flights to buy, and Oscar was paying a large sum of alimony each month. I would tease him and say that before we married, I looked at the asset side of the balance sheet and thought I did pretty well, but I forgot to look at the liability side. Anyway, the sales people didn't hover, but they were right there offering to let me try on anything I wanted. There was one ring that caught my eye. It was a one-caret baguette emerald with four diamonds in a swirl of yellow gold. Mari encouraged me. She eyed the sales person with a look that asked "Is that the best price you can offer?"

I never bought something like this without Oscar. Hell, I had never bought anything like this, period! A few hours later I headed back to the ship with my souvenir. Oscar was happy that I found something and took great delight in my excitement. He wanted to show me the world and give me everything in it. *Do I have to wake up from this dream? I feel like a princess. When is this carriage going to turn back into a pumpkin? I can't believe my good fortune, the dresses, the shoes, the dancing, the ships and a prince that adores me. Thank you, God.*

A short time later, Oscar was laid off from his VP of Operations job at the cruise line. They gave him six months' severance pay so we weren't too worried. I was working at a huge law firm in downtown Miami in their litigation department, but it wasn't a good fit. I wasn't happy there, so I looked for something closer to home in Fort Lauderdale. Luck would bring me to a great attorney practicing real estate law who shared his infectious love of local history. He and his wife also loved to travel so they understood when I needed spontaneous time off to accompany Oscar. It was a perfect match.

Soon after I took the new job, we went to a maritime convention in New York. Oscar had meetings during the day and I kept myself busy. The second day he called and asked me to meet him in the lobby for cocktails. I went down and waited. In the 10 minutes I was waiting, several men wandered over to me and congratulated me. I politely thanked them, having no idea why.

When Oscar finally arrived, I asked him, "Why have people been congratulating me?"

"I'm sorry. I wanted to be the first to tell you. I accepted a position today as VP of Operations."

"Wow, honey that's great!"

"Well, the only thing is that the company is based in New Jersey."

My mind was racing. *What is he saying?*

"What? What?" I think I went into shock. It had only been a short time since I relocated from Texas to Florida. While they had been adventurous, exciting years, they were also stressful and heart-wrenching. We had just purchased our first home in a very nice suburb of Fort Lauderdale and remodeled the entire inside with new paint, carpet and furniture, art deco style. I didn't want to move.

Our courtship was long-distance before I moved to Florida. I proposed the same now. "How about I stay in Florida and you go to New Jersey? We just finished the house. I have a great new job. Your children are in Florida."

He agreed. We decided he would commute back and forth on the weekends and so we began another long-distance relationship, only this time as newlyweds.

He began his new job promptly. Bermuda Star Line was a very different organization. He was told he'd have to wear a suit to work every day, preferably a 3-piece suit and no cowboy boots allowed. Oscar loved his cowboy boots. He began living in a hotel and coming home to Florida on the weekends. That lasted about eight months, until he called me one day and said, "Corporate jobs require my wife to accompany me. You have to join me in New Jersey."

I knew he was right, and besides, I missed him terribly. I quit my job, packed up and sold the house. New Jersey here I come! We made an adventure out of it, of course. Leah and Nathan came for one of their visits, and friends helped us caravan from Ft. Lauderdale to New Jersey. We arrived safe and sound and got down to the business of settling in.

We rented a dirty old house, because it was all we could find that allowed us to keep the trailer out front. We all started cleaning, as I laid out the rules. "Pops has a ship leaving New York for Bermuda in one week. We can go on that cruise, if we get this house clean and settled." We worked hard and one week later we sailed out of the port of New York. We drove into the city early enough for a carriage ride around Central Park and lunch at a famous deli and then we were onboard, Bermuda-bound. Another adventure. *Dreams can come true.*

A short time later one of Oscar's ships was making a repositioning cruise. It would be 21 days from San Francisco going through the Panama Canal.

"I can't go, but you can," he said.

I packed for the daily touring, the beaches and the dressy evening attire. I took three large suitcases so I could have a different outfit for each of the 21 nights. Oscar said he'd join me in the middle of the itinerary for about 5 days. We flew to San Francisco and spent a few romantic days there and then he helped me board the ship and settle in. Oscar kissed me goodbye and he was off. I'd see him in about 10 days. *OMG. Don't be scared Adrienne. It's OK to be by yourself.*

I explored the ship and unpacked. The second night on the ship there was a singles mingle. *Hum—I am alone. Does that mean I'm single? Absolutely.* I went and as I sat there, one by one, three different handsome men approached me for conversation. All of a sudden, we were a group of four. We were the only ones onboard under the age of 70. They were in their 50's. I was still in my 30's. They wondered why their travel agent would book them on a cruise where the average age was dead. They should have known that not many folks in their 50's can afford the time or money to take a 21-day cruise. One owned a winery in the Napa Valley. One was a real estate broker in Beverly Hills and one was a doctor in southern California. I explained that I was very happily married, but my husband would be glad I had someone to entertain me.

So, for the next ten days we were travel mates. There was parasailing, taxies, restaurants, dancing, tours and lots of fun. It was a very nice trip, but 21 days is a long time and I really wasn't that impressed with going through the Panama Canal. I know it's on a bucket list for many people but this was my second time and I still wasn't that impressed. The best part was that we were headed to Colombia. Yup—as soon as we docked in Cartagena, I took a taxi to the same little jewelry store and purchased a marquis drop emerald to wear as a pendant necklace. Ah—another souvenir. *No t-shirts for me.* In the Caribbean I bought gold and rubies but Cartagena was for emeralds.

I was comfortable at sea, finding it relaxing, energizing and empowering. I was feeling like I could say hello to God again. I wanted to have a conversation with Him without being so angry.

For the first time in a while, I thought that maybe the bad stuff wasn't His fault at all.

Always seeking out times to connect with family, we flew one of Oscar's daughters from Florida to New York to join us for a cruise to Bermuda. It was the three of us and we spent some time with the captain and his crew. One evening we sat down with the captain and a few of the officers for cocktails before dinner. We decided to order shots, since she loved shots. I loved B-52's. They were a sweet concoction, which was not her usual drink, but sure—why not. Oscar did not do shots. In this circle of folks all dressed up for dinner, she and I lifted our glasses in a toast, tilted our heads back and downed the layered sweetness. We looked at each other and immediately I saw horror in her eyes. The drink did not go all the way down. She clasped her hands together like a bucket under her nose to catch the liquid pouring out. She ran to the restroom. I felt so bad for her. We didn't drink any shots the rest of the cruise. Despite the little incident, we had a great time and chuckled. It was so nice to be able to give her an adventure and use this time for building new relationships.

We were in New Jersey only a few months when I knew it was time to settle down and think about work. I was thinking about a new program in the legal field. I had been a legal secretary now for 7 or 8 years, and it might be time to take it up a notch. Paralegal training was becoming popular. When I called Tom and asked what he thought, he liked the idea. I enrolled at a local college for a paralegal degree. It meant no travel while I attended the one-year course, but it would be worth it.

Meanwhile, Oscar didn't like his job at the cruise line. There were three ships under his control and he was responsible for the ship's safety and the safety of the passengers, as well as the thousands of crew who worked on those ships. He was drinking a bottle of Mylanta a day. Oscar cared mostly about his ships and his crews. He didn't like corporate politics. Behind the scenes in the office part of the job, there were some things going on that bothered him. He talked about leaving the job, but what would we do?

I was attending paralegal school and our monthly budget was high. His first wife was receiving alimony for life. He needed that job.

Then on Easter, 1988, the phone rang in the middle of the night. It's not usually a good thing when the phone rings in the middle of the night. Oscar listened. Holding the phone away from his ear, he turned to me and said, "Get me a beer." He didn't say a word as he listened and I was clueless. When he hung up the phone, he asked for another beer, and then he finally spoke. "That was Ma." She said his ex-wife had remarried several months earlier, but no one wanted to tell him. Another secret kept.

"You know what this means?"

"No, what?" I asked.

"No more alimony payments."

Let that sink in.

When Oscar got divorced, he offered his ex-wife the moon. After all, they had been married 28 years and had 7 children together. He was being fair and he was going to marry a much younger woman. He offered her a college education, health and life insurance and half his pension; if something happened to him and all the assets would be hers, all the debts would be his. She didn't want that. She wanted alimony for the rest of her life. He tried to tell her that she was receiving bad advice, but she wouldn't listen. Alimony forever and child support for now, as well as all the assets and no debts—that's what she wanted, and the judge agreed. She did not realize that if she remarried the alimony would stop.

This would change everything. Oscar had choices now. Only a few days later, he had asked if we could afford for him to quit his job.

"Of course, darling," I said, "we'll figure it out."

He stayed on for a little while so I could finish my degree.

When Oscar handed in his resignation and the president of the cruise line asked him where he was going, Oscar was so happy to say, "I'm going camping."

That was the beginning of the next adventure. It was time to take a pilgrimage. Oscar needed to figure out what he wanted to do with the rest of his life. He was only 52 years old. He needed a respite, and the open road was calling. We planned a route and pin-pointed a place in Idaho where my children would join us. When we headed out, it was time to unplug—no computers, no phones and little TV. We'd check in along the way at payphones. We had maps and music. We had each other. He had his books and I had a new hobby. My daughter just taught me counted cross-stitch. It was relaxing and meditative. Oscar did 90% of the driving and I would stitch. We always made sure I could handle driving any rig we owned. I needed to be a relief driver. We drove miles with comfortable silence or we'd listen to our eclectic choices of music as I stitched away. Little did I know that simple hobby would be the beginning of a new passion that would grow for the rest of my life. I loved a needle and thread.

We drove out of Florida heading west. The mountains and the outdoors were filled with God's presence. Peace was filling us up. We didn't pack any Mylanta. We stopped for one week camping inside Yellowstone National Park. We saw Old Faithful and hiked learning a lot on our daily ranger guided tours.

One evening, getting ready for an early-to-bed night, there was a pounding on the door. Oscar wrangled on some clothes to open the door. There were floodlights pointed at our camper and a loud speaker announced "Ranger Rogers here. Do you know there are no coolers allowed outside your camper?"

"Yes sir, we do, but that large one is empty."

"Well, the bears don't know that. You have to bring that cooler inside."

"OK."

"You don't understand. I mean before I leave, I need to see that cooler removed."

The rest of the week on each of our tours, we looked for Ranger Rogers, hoping to see him again.

We were looking forward to my children joining us in Idaho and reconnecting for a visit with an old shipmate of Oscar's, Ed Price. We rode horses and arranged for Nathan and Ed to take a ride in a biplane. Then we headed to the Oregon coast and its amazing scenery. We moved onward south down the western coast of the US toward Yosemite National Park. Those majestic massive mountains of my childhood grab my soul. Also, I wanted Oscar and the children to have the opportunity to hug the massive redwoods. Everyone should hug a redwood.

More family time was waiting for us in the San Diego area to visit with my brothers. It was great to see them and for them to see my children. They also were a bit envious of our ability to take some time for wanderlust. The story goes that my sister-in-law was so taken by all the cute RV accessories, such as the tiny collapsible dish drainer, that shortly later they bought a camper. We might have been a bad influence on them.

It was time to start heading back east again. We made arrangements with the children's step mom, Kayla, to join us camping in San Antonio and pick up the children. Not long after my divorce, my ex had announced that he was going to propose to someone. I asked him if she knew about his secret. He assured me she did. I thought she was a better woman than I to be able to look past his urges. When they married, I was happy for them and happy that my children had a woman in their home. She was gracious in always helping to make sure the children called, sent me letters and were available for our visitations. It was she, not my ex, who coordinated everything for our visits. We became friends. In fact, Oscar and I gave her and her friend a cruise on one of his ships. When we were coordinating the return of the children from our summer trip, it was perfect to plan for us to rendezvous in San Antonio and spend some time together.

During that visit, she asked me, "Why didn't you tell me?"

"Tell you what?" I asked.

"About his wishing he was a woman."

OMG. I told her I asked him and he said he told her before they married. He didn't, though—she found out after they were married. The difference was that her marriage was not arranged. She loved him and was determined to work it out. She stayed with him twenty years. I respected her for being more open-minded than me. My relationship with her was complicated by my insecurities and yet it was simple. We loved the same children and we shared the unusual circumstance of both having been married to a man who wished he was a woman.

When it was time to head home, we didn't hurry. We meandered home to Fort Lauderdale. We'd been gone more than three months exploring and recharging. While we had children with us some of the time and stopped along the way to see friends and family, it was mostly a time to connect with each other without the distractions of daily life. We loved the intimate time of being together, looking through the lens as a couple and yet still respecting our individuality. We confirmed that space was irrelevant to us. We didn't need a lot of it. We were comfortable in our small space. We were comfortable in our silences. We were comfortable in sharing the stories of our past with each other. We were each grateful for someone to see us, listen to us, care about us. We had each travelled a lonely life and now we had each other.

That trip would set the stage for decades to come. We shared a mutual conviction that travel broadens one's view. We were passionate about exploring and adventure. Being able to spend time with the ocean and the mountains and the forests touched our souls. It was no longer a dream, but a compulsion and a passion. We would plan the rest of our lives accordingly, pursuing the possibilities and adventures that lay just around the corner.

One of my young sons-in-law once told me that I expected too much, which set me up for disappointments. There is a bit of truth to that. I never wanted the children to feel they were not enough. On the other hand, I strongly believe that an individual has the power and ability to design their own dreams. It's important to dream and work on making that dream a reality. It's important to develop the ability to get back up when you fall, and keep dreaming—always dreaming.

Spaces

Home from the sojourn, we were rested, open and ready to see what the next phase of life looked like. I found another great job, and I felt so lucky that what I needed seemed to always magically appear behind Door #1 whenever I knocked. There was a sign that sat on my desk for many years that read: "To the person who has achieved inner clarity, new paths appear and doors open without the need to knock." However, I was never afraid to knock.

Oscar and I settled into regular 9-5 working schedules, saving the weekends for adventures. We discovered an RV golf resort in central Florida, and after some consideration, we bought a 1,000 square foot prefabricated home there. It was really a decked-out single-wide trailer on the 14th fairway, and served as a very nice vacation home. Now we had our place in southern Florida, our RV and our vacation home in central Florida. The family loved vacationing at the central Florida place where they could ride bikes and golf carts around the 2,800-acre RV resort or swim in the Olympic-size swimming pool.

We were living a wonderful life. I found a job I liked and Oscar was doing contract work surveying cruise ships. Often when he went to inspect the ships I tagged along. We realized that maybe we didn't need two homes and an RV so we thought about selling one of the homes and realized we'd rather make our main home in central Florida, closer to where the children had moved. Thinking it might take a while to sell our south Florida place we went ahead

Glamor shot, 1992

and listed it. We were wrong—it sold right away. *Now what are we going to do? I'm not really quite ready to quit my job and relocate yet.* Finally, I said it out loud, "Well, we do have a camper. We can set it up at a campground in Fort Lauderdale until we decide on our timing for relocation."

Every foot you have or don't have in an RV counts. It was time to upgrade from our 24' trailer. We ended up with a top of the line, fully equipped 40' Royals International with double slides and a washer/dryer. During the week we lived there in our 320 square feet of trailer space. On the weekends we visited our spacious 1,000 square foot resort home. Neither of us minded small spaces—Oscar lived on ships and I had lived in small spaces during my commune days. I suppose we were ahead of our time, since now there is an entire movement of tiny home people. After four years of that arrangement, however, it was time to relocate, take the risk, and find another job. So, we moved out of the RV into our 1,000 square foot park model on the golf course in a lovely resort. It was the life of Riley.

I've never felt like I needed a lot of physical space to live in. I don't need a big kitchen or acres or lots of square footage. The space that is important to me is in my mind. I need the mental space to plan for travel and be still for prayer and meditation in order to find clarity. I need space for the creative ventures in my life, which require thought. Luckily, I married a man who is on the same page as me, not needing physical space to be comfortable. We needed space in our calendar to stand on a shoreline or on a ship and see endless water reflecting vast open spaces. We both wanted space in our calendars, our hearts and our budgets to look out over a mountain range with its endless expanse. We didn't need a big home because the space we wanted most lies within us.

There is one thing about living in small spaces, though—it works better when everything is organized. Sometime in my forties, I began to recognize my OCD. I've never been clinically diagnosed but the symptoms are obvious. Yes—I like everything in order. No, it's not just that I like it that way. It must be in order for me to have peace. I like objects in order. I like budgets balanced. I like schedules kept. Lack of order creates chaos and stress. A friend once told me there are drugs for this condition, but I don't want drugs to fix it. I get so much done in my life. I make the most of every minute of every day. Even when I'm sitting doing nothing, I view it as valuable time to recharge so that I can tackle the next thing. I love how much I accomplish in my life. I'm grateful that my obsession is not so severe that I turn the stove off 20 times or relock the door 20 times, but I am compulsive about finishing things and maintaining organization. I need order to keep pace with the demands of life. I spend time every morning at my desk organizing papers, budgets and calendars and correspondence. Once that is all done, my mind has free space for dreaming and time to pursue my passions and to play. It's a self-imposed reward strategy, but it's not a choice, it's a compulsion. If things are out of order, it's like a rattle shaking continually inside of me getting louder and louder—it's very annoying and I can't settle down. It can be a blessing and a curse, for sure. I know it sounds strange and I suppose there are times I wish I could let it go, but mostly I'm comfortable with my obsession for order. With my home and my life organized, I'm always ready to follow my dreams, be creative and go on an adventure.

We were always on some adventure. There were cruises and RV trips and friends and family. This one time...we took a ride to visit my old commune property. It was a beautiful ride up the Blue Ridge Parkway. The property was now inhabited by other people, but for me the people of The Way, The Truth and the Life came alive again that day. The sanctuary was now a rundown junk shop called Fast Eddies. We stepped up onto the porch to peek into the windows. I touched the door handle and found it unlocked. No one was there. I looked in Oscar's eyes and saw a warning to be careful. His look said, "Watch your step and your heart."

I pushed the door open, needing to walk in that space. The main area wasn't accessible, but the storage area was open. I went inside. Once before in my life, I'd walked into a room to make a big discovery and I had the same feeling overwhelming me now. I was stepping back in time. There was stuff heaped everywhere in disarray. Some 50 feet in I stopped in my tracks. There was my daughter's baby carriage. Emotions flooded me. The gloom and oppression of the commune lay heavy on me.

When I finally emerged from the building and Oscar took my hand, I felt his surge of strength and the power of overcoming and returning in time to the now. The restaurant turned dining room was once again a restaurant. It was lunch time so we went in and sat down. It was so bizarre. Oscar told them I had been one of the commune girls who lived there. The owners heard a lot of stories.

This would not be the last time for me to return to the old commune property. I knew I would need to walk those grounds again several times in my life.

Although we weren't parents or grandparents cheering at weekly school events or hosting regular Sunday dinners, we did love to take our grandchildren on trips with us. We wanted them to see a bigger picture of the world and its boundaries. We made space in our calendar and our budget to travel and connect with family and friends to maintain many long-distance relationships. Sometimes a birthday or Christmas was a way to give that treat. I was always wanting to find the perfect gift for people. One year I gave Oscar horseback riding lessons. One year the girls all got beautiful gold from the Caribbean. There were watches and cameras.

One of the most memorable gifts required coordination and cooperation from one of my step-daughters. I called her and told her my idea. She agreed to have our grandson available for the event and the plan was hatched. I made the reservations. That year Oscar's Christmas gift was that he and our grandson Eddie, then 7, would attend Space Camp for 3 nights at Cape Canaveral. It was a huge bonding experience and I believe it changed both of their lives forever. They explored space and experienced "zero gravity" and shared time alone, just the two of them.

We took two of our grandchildren on a 3-night cruise when they were around 5 and 8. They had such a good time dressing up and dancing and learning table manners. We always loved our time with grandchildren without their parents. Don't get me wrong, we love the parents too, but generally speaking the kids are better behaved and open up more when their parents are not around.

When we were home and not travelling, our life at the resort was very nice. I was the baby in every social group, since most of our friends were closer to Oscar's age. The retired folks there played bridge. When they found out I learned as a child, they were happy to take me in and let me refresh my memory. Bridge is a great way to exercise your mind and have social interaction. It's helped me make new friends whenever and wherever we moved. The fellowship among the folks is warm and I only play a friendly game. You hear about the serious cutthroat players, but my friends and I are always good sports.

The ships were always calling to Oscar. He loved being an inspector, but he kept his ear to the ground for another job working for a cruise line. He received a phone call informing him that Disney Cruise Line was looking for a Vice President of Marine Operations. He sent his resume. They scheduled an interview. That day I waited anxiously for him to get home and to hear how it went.

"Well?" I asked.

"I didn't get the position," he replied.

"What happened? Tell me everything."

Calm as a cucumber, he said, "Everything was going very well and then one of the interviewers said, "Before we talk money, we need to let you know something—Disney does not allow beards. You'd have to shave."

"So, what did you say?"

"I simply closed my portfolio and pushed back my chair and said thank you very much gentlemen, but I guess this interview is over."

OMG—this husband of mine. He didn't even ask how much money was being offered. He just knew he didn't want to work for a company that would be in that much control over his personal attire. He'd been there, done that.

There were also some sad times during this period. Oscar was working with his beloved mentor, Captain Hofstra, when his wife Jenny had a massive stroke that left her mind OK, but not one part of her body cooperated. She lived that way for 2 years before she passed. It was a long journey and Oscar was there every day with Captain Hofstra. To me this was further proof of the loyalty I had first seen in this honorable man I married. When Jenny passed, they would visit her grave every week for years. This made a huge impression on Oscar.

Captain Hofstra was up in years with failing health and a short time after we moved to central Florida, he passed away too. An amazing thing happened. Although they had no formal or written agreement about the fate of the business, his sons knew how their father felt about Oscar and the support Oscar had been to him for so many years. They gave Oscar full access to all the business files and handed the business to Oscar on a handshake. While it was a sad, sad time for Oscar, he would have his ships. We just had to hold on to each other a little more closely.

Oscar was a religious Catholic who never missed church. We made the space on our calendar every Sunday for church. I was starting to think more about God as a loving father, who would want only the best for his children. *God, you must be smiling at our marriage*. We tried a Baptist church, but with their loud preaching and weekly altar calls, it was a little too much like the commune for me and Oscar really didn't like it. We settled on attending Catholic services. It felt safe to me as I could listen without being really engaged. It might have taken years but my heart was softening to God. When we moved to central Florida, however, we didn't find a church home. We were faithful, we just were not churched. It made the losses we experienced harder. While the commune was an extreme and distorted belief system of church community, I do believe community plays an important part in the support of our faith journey and our daily strength and purpose.

As time marched on, Oscar's kids were getting married, having children, getting divorced and growing up. Leah and Nathan were both in college now. Oscar's business took off and he was busier than ever. He worked from home to prepare for the arrival of a ship and its Coast Guard inspections and required certificates. He would then travel to visit the ship and conduct the inspection or safety training required. I was working at a law firm in downtown Orlando. I found my way to a senior partner, doing estate and tax planning law. The commute was an hour each way plus the job required 8-10 hours of daily work, which made for very long days. We were in the grind, building back up our financial reserves so that we could take the next adventure.

One day the phone rang and I was alarmed but pleased to hear my children's stepmother, Kayla, on the other end of the line. She said she needed to tell me something. It had been years since that day in San Antonio when she told me she knew that my children's father desired to be a woman. All these years, on occasion, he would experiment. I knew it from the times I saw him with plucked eyebrows and his nails a little longer. By now his wanting to be a woman didn't threaten my womanhood and while I still didn't understand his transgender desires, it didn't bother me so much. He seemed to be managing his double life. His mother would tell me sometimes, "I'm watching him for you." She thought that if the secret came out it would change everything. When Mimi passed away, I believe not having her there profoundly changed him. Kayla said he had announced he wanted to begin living as a woman. He didn't say he wanted surgery or anything. He just didn't want to hide anymore. He wanted to wear women's clothes and makeup and embrace his female side. She wanted a divorce. While it would be hard to tell Leah and Nathan, who were in college now, it might be harder to tell their half-brother, Kayla's son, who was only 13 at the time. Kayla told my ex that he had to be the one to tell all three children. She was calling to tell me the secret was out. They would know now. I should have felt better not to have to carry this secret any longer, but I didn't. I was full of fear.

Nathan came right away for a visit to talk about his feelings about all this. His faith probably served him the best among us because he has always been able to be fully accepting of others, free of judgment. It was a little more difficult for Leah, maybe because she is female. Perhaps she felt like she was protecting the honor of her mom and stepmom. Perhaps she was angry about the years of deception. We all had a jungle of emotions to navigate.

We made a few more trips back to Dallas for visits. On one occasion we went to see my mentor, Tom and his wife, to catch up. He was still, and always would be, watching out for me, his baby bird with broken wings.

"Perhaps it's time to come back to Dallas," he suggested. He and his wife had just purchased a home on 40 acres in Celina, Texas, which is a rural suburb of Dallas. He made an offer. Touring me around the old ranch house with a pond behind it he said,

"Bobbie would prefer to build a new house on a ridge in the back. How about you and Oscar buy this house from me with an access easement, of course, and ya'll come share the property and then you come run my court." By then Tom was a judge.

Wow, what an offer. I told him, "We'll think about it."

Oscar and I discussed it. Running a court sounded scary to me and beyond my qualifications. Oscar said he would always feel like it was Tom's place. Not even a piece of it would really ever feel his own. Besides, Oscar was still working with his beloved ships, and moving to Dallas, which wasn't near a port, would surely end his career. In the end we declined Tom's gracious offer. It did water the seed that had lain dormant for many years: my need to return to Dallas to be closer to my children.

In 1999 we came to Dallas for another visit and then drove 200 miles south to Willis, Texas to visit Oscar's uncle. Uncle Bud was also a man of the sea. He was how and why Oscar found his way to escape the car plants of Detroit. Uncle Bud and Aunt Joann lived in a wonderful home overlooking Lake Conroe. It was just thirty miles from Houston, which was considered a port city. We shared a few days of visiting and telling stories, and Aunt Joann encouraged us to move near them, to Willis. On the third morning, standing upstairs gazing out over the lake, Oscar said softly, "I think I could live here."

Without another word, when we returned home the next week, I put a For Sale sign in the front yard. We were Texas-bound.

Again, it was a risk. Oscar wasn't sure his business would follow him to Texas. Most of his ships were calling on Florida ports, to which he could drive. Once we lived in Texas, they would have to be willing to fly him to the port and pay for travel days. But we decided the benefits out-weighed the risks. We were hopeful for a sale, a move and a future woven more closely with *my* children.

Then Oscar's son Gerard came for a visit from Okinawa. His twenty-year Marine Corps career was almost up. He asked if he could land at our place at the golf resort with his wife and toddler. Although our place was a mere 1,000 square feet, we said of course, we would figure it out. Excited to meet our granddaughter, we put the sale and the move on hold. We put some portable cabinets in the living room so they'd have a space for their things.

Oscar was excited for this time of reunion with Gerard. As boys, Gerard and his older brother spent a lot of quality time with Oscar, as they were Boy Scouts and Oscar was a Boy Scout leader. They loved to camp and do the outdoor adventures and both boys worked hard for their many merit badges. They also worked on cars together, mostly out of necessity; but it was a good bonding and teaching experience for Oscar with his sons. Together they tore apart and rebuilt an engine or two and learned how to do the handyman things required around a home. While Oscar was a mere 5'9," both sons grew to be over 6' tall. The Poppe men all have those handsome strong cheekbones, good hair and light eyes. Gerard was no different—tall, good-looking, lean and strong from all his years in the military. It was touching to see the resemblance between father and son. We hadn't seen a lot of Gerard over the years, because he served most of his time in the military overseas.

Gerard arrived with his wife and our granddaughter and only a few possessions. He would never really discuss his job in the Marines, but he was an expert marksman and served much of his time in jungles and places he couldn't divulge. A dad now, he was smitten and in love with his dear daughter, who was beautiful and sweet natured. His wife wasn't happy from day one. I don't think she wanted to move to the United States. They drank a lot. One time a neighbor asked Oscar to do something about it.

"What do you mean?" Oscar asked.

"He is standing out back of your house and yelling in a drunken rage at the golfers," was the reply.

Oscar told Gerard he had to stop. Oscar assumed Gerard had been overindulging because he was decompressing from the military and getting used to being in new surroundings. The officer in Oscar thought he could just issue the order and it would be followed. However, this was more than decompressing. This was an addiction. Gerard was not capable of just following that order.

Other times, I would arrive home from work to find everything in the kitchen cabinets in disarray. Bored, his wife was trying to help by rearranging. Communicating was difficult because she spoke no English and was usually tipsy at the very least. I would talk and Gerard would interpret. It was stressful for each of us for different reasons.

One day I came home from work and they were both sitting on the floor with an open bottle of booze and our granddaughter running wildly in circles. I'm sure they were all just playing and waiting for me to fix dinner, but something about the scene was unsettling. *If only I could go back in time, I would get back in the car and drive somewhere, anywhere and not have said anything to anyone, especially not to Oscar.* Instead, I told Oscar we could not continue this way if they could not curtail their drinking.

Don't get me wrong, I like to party and I could keep up with the best of them, but there is a time and place for everything. This was not the time or the place. Oscar was travelling, but said he'd talk to Gerard when he got home a few days later. To this day I don't know what was said. For a short time, Gerard continued to stay with us but moved his wife and daughter to a hotel, thinking that perhaps a little break would help everyone. Their excessive drinking continued. Oscar told them the arrangements were not going to work. They moved in with Oscar's sister, who lived one town over. When they had a son, they came to visit so that we could see our granddaughter and our new grandson.

Then his wife decided she would not stay in the US any longer. They all returned to Okinawa, but in the end, she divorced Gerard and the government said he couldn't stay there if he wasn't married, so he returned to the States, divorced and without his children. He was so depressed, understandably. I knew the pain of losing children, but I did not understand alcoholism. Gerard was bitter and angry and sad. He used alcohol as a painkiller to dull his grief.

In reality alcohol is a depressant and it just perpetuated the cycle of hopelessness. Perhaps he blamed us for his wife not wanting to stay in the US. I don't know. For whatever reason, a very painful estrangement from Gerard began. He would call from time to time, but only when he was drunk. We continued to tell him we loved him and wanted to see him, and continued to send cards and gifts. Although while he was in the Marines and lived overseas, we didn't see him for long stretches at a time, this estrangement was different and confusing. Certainly, the future Oscar and I hoped to build together with Gerard and his family was lost.

Knowing that Gerard was struggling and hostile, we tried to make ourselves indifferent to the loss, but we knew that our bond with him was broken. We tried to bury the pain deep in our hearts, praying for reconciliation with Gerard and with his family. It was like an impending storm hovering over our hearts. He was Oscar's son, but it had been my job to make him love me. I had failed. A darkness settled over a portion of our hearts, but we continued to reach for the light. We needed to carry on and move forward. It's what I do. It's what Oscar does. We needed to recover from this storm. And so we resumed our plan to move to Texas.

Deep in the Heart of Texas

In December of 1999, even though our Florida home was not sold, we made up our minds to leave anyway. Deciding to sell the house furnished, we kept only a few important pieces of furniture and all our memorabilia. With the familiar U-Haul truck in the driveway, I certainly was in touch with the fact that I was channeling my parents—able to pick up and move, again and again.

We dug deep and found that hope still lived in our hearts. In Texas we would not only be closer to my children, we'd be close to Oscar's beloved Uncle Bud, and we'd also be in a central location, perfect for exploring the US by RV. Oscar and I spent time talking about the pros and cons of a move and making sure we were both on the same page about the process. Our life in Texas would have possibilities. Somewhere I read that a satisfying life requires strategy, daily attention, self-awareness and discipline. I was intentional in my deep-seated desire to relocate to Texas.

We had a few mishaps along the way, but we would not be deterred. At last we were on our way, with a friend to help us caravan, a U-haul truck, our car and our 4-door Silverado truck towing our 5th wheel trailer. The 5th wheel trailer is designed to extend over the bed of the truck and hitches into the truck bed, acting like a 5th wheel to the truck. It's a more secure ride because the trailer becomes one with the truck. Oscar loved his 5th wheel and it was quite roomy when the slide-out rooms were extended opening up to a spacious 300 square feet.

Arriving in Texas, we rented an RV site in the area where we wanted to live and set ourselves up so we could shop for a home. I wanted to see Lake Conroe from my back window, but Oscar said maintaining a bulkhead is too expensive. He wanted to spend our disposable money on travel. There was a subdivision that really appealed to me. We went and talked to the President of the Homeowner's Association about whether it was OK to have an RV parked in the driveway. It was permitted in certain sections.

"What are you looking for?" the HOA president asked. We had no particulars about the house itself in mind, but we wanted space for the RV, guest parking and, of course, we had a certain budget. He told us he knew of a couple who were thinking of selling. The house was only two years old and the couple were RV-ers, so there was an RV pad with hook ups for electricity and water right alongside the house.

We drove by it. It was a 2-story home set on two residential lots with a 3rd empty lot on one side and a greenbelt on the other side and behind it. There were a lot of beautiful mature trees. The setting was really nice. My heart racing, I looked at Oscar, shrugged my shoulders and went and knocked on their door.

When Mr. Parker answered I told him, "We are looking for a house and we heard you might be interested in selling. "

"We haven't decided to sell," he said.

"Just in case, may we come in and look?" I asked.

He opened the door and said, "Come on in."

I didn't love the floor plan with its small rooms and the galley kitchen with no window. But it had a cozy screened porch like our Florida home. Oscar loved the roomy two and a half car garage and the RV pad alongside the house.

The following week we asked if we could go back and look again. My friend Kathy came down from Dallas and walked the house with me. We could all see a life for us in that place, so we made an offer. OMG. They accepted.

When we closed on our place in Willis, Texas, it felt like we had stepped into the light, especially since the perfect house just appeared on our path. It was a quaint two-story home with 3 bedrooms and

2 bathrooms. It was 1,700 square feet, which is considered small by Texas standards, but it was a big contrast to the 1,000 square feet we left in Florida. It also had a lovely front porch with rocking chairs, plus the RV was right there so Oscar could tinker with it all the time and it served as additional guest quarters. We could welcome family and friends for visits with plenty of room.

Grandson and great-grandkids, visiting us in Texas.

Every day we have choices of who we want to be and where we want to go. We can design our dreams like an artist or quilter designs a piece of art. We envisioned this move, made a plan, took action and now here we were, ready to develop our dream life. I heard my mother's voice reminding me, "You bring yourself wherever you go."

Please Lord, I want to embrace all of myself, the good, the bad and the ugly. Help me to put my best foot forward. I want to forgive my shortcomings and embrace my strengths. Help me just to be myself.

Roots

The first few years in Willis were magical. We were only 200 miles south of Dallas, where my children, Leah and Nathan, and my friend Tom and my dear friend Kathy lived. We'd take the RV to Tom's ranch in Celina and join the family festivities. We loved being there. Everyone loved being there. Bobbie is the ultimate hostess and as an interior designer, she created a place that was warm, elegant and inviting. She is also a wonderful gardener. I learned so much from watching and listening to her. Tom and Oscar also adored each other and we loved the intimate times we enjoyed with them sitting on the back porch or huddled around the fire sharing our stories.

This one time...we were visiting at Tom and Bobbie's ranch, which they called Celestial Celina, and Tom had a project for Oscar to help him undertake. He said, "Come on—we're gonna get those beavers." Some beavers had taken up residence in the pond behind the house, and were nibbling away at Bobbie's trees on the far side of the pond, making more than an appetizer of those trees. None of the officials were having any luck in catching the beavers for release somewhere else. The traps were not working, so Tom decided he was going to take care of them. He had a plan. OMG. One night Oscar and Tom took two chairs down by the pond. Oscar manned the flashlight and Tom manned the shotgun, while they waited in the dark. Those two guys, who had spent time together smoking cigars and mending fences, were now on a crazy mission to kill those pesky beavers. We heard the shots and hoped everything was OK. They didn't get even one beaver, but they did shoot the hell out of those trees. Well, it had been a good plan—maybe if they had been a little younger, with better eyes and steadier hands. We sure laughed a lot.

It brought me great joy to open our Texas home and make an inviting place for gatherings. Everyone came to Willis for visits. We loved taking our RV west to the Texas hill country for further exploration. The warmth of the light as we stepped into Texas filled our hearts and radiated out, bringing new friends to our path. One day at the community pool, a woman started up a conversation, aware that we were new to the area.

"Do you play cards?" she asked.

"I play bridge, but my husband doesn't," I told her.

"Well, we have a women's bridge group and perhaps we can play a different game to include your husband," she said.

"We'd love that," I replied.

It wasn't long before she called and invited us. That would begin one of the deepest, most loving woman friendships of my life. My dear, dear friend Darlene is 30 years my senior. She is fun-loving, kind, smart, thoughtful, strong, sincere and the best listener I've ever known. It was so much fun getting to know each other. We were honest and real with each other. She grew up in a one-room house with a lot of children and appreciated just how far she'd come, taking nothing for granted. Darlene and Al had a home on the lake and she loved to entertain, as well as to dance. She introduced me to her circle of women friends and their husbands. Oscar liked the men. He had been keeping men at a distance, since so many of his friends passed away in the last few years, but these men were different, and a few were also former military. He let them in. We talked about house projects and travel, played Mexican Train dominos and went to local places in small groups to dance.

We became close friends with Jim and Shirley, fellow RV-ers. Radiating a warm smile, my beloved Shirley was one of the sweetest, kindest people I would ever know. She had three sons, so she learned to love football and fishing and boy did she love her sports, fishing and her dogs. She loved to travel and loved all kinds of crafts. Around this time, a next-door neighbor of mine introduced me to the art of scrapbooking, and Shirley was interested. I wanted to start keeping albums, diary-style, one for each year—documenting our travels and also daily events like washing the RV or laying rocks at the house. Shirley wanted to make albums for her sons' birthdays. We'd scrapbook together all day, sharing supplies while having wonderful warm conversation. Shirley brought out the best in me.

Other good friends from this time included Lise and Ron, who were both well-educated and well-travelled. We would gather all four couples together on a regular basis for games or dancing or conversation. Lise was great at entertaining and was a great cook too. I watched and learned from these women and their strong, spirited husbands and soon my confidence grew. I found that I too loved entertaining and had a natural knack for this new art. Making the house and food ready for conversation and fellowship energized me. The fact that these folks were so appreciative of the art of entertaining made it even more fun. They noticed the details and effort. Ten for dinner at our little place was crowded, but they didn't care—if I called and said I was cooking, they came.

Whenever I had an elaborate sit-down dinner planned, it would begin ten days before the big day. I would drag out cookbooks and sit and look through them. I read cookbooks like novels. Some have stories scattered throughout, sharing the history of the recipe. To this day, my personal 3-ring binder filled with recipes brings back fond memories of family and friends and events at which we shared the meals made from those recipes. For a party, I had to plan the appetizers for cocktail hour, a salad, the main course and dessert. "Bring an appetite" was always the theme. I have a few standards for my appetizers, almost always making artichoke dip and spinach roll ups. Depending on the crowd I'll make my mother's chopped liver, which folks either love or hate. Once a friend falls in love with it, I find I have to make it every time they come to my home. The house must be stocked with wine and a full bar.

None of us were big drinkers, but I wanted my guests to be able to have the cocktail of their choice.

Once the menu is planned and the shopping is done, it's time to plan the cooking. I like to make as much as I can the day before, like the dips and dressings. I wake up very early the morning of a dinner party so that I can clean house and set the table. Since our Willis house was quite small, we could not all congregate in one place. Folks would take turns moving around the buffet of appetizers set in the kitchen, while the laundry room, just off the kitchen, was converted into the bar with a tablecloth across the washer and dryer, to break up the crowd a bit.

I would also pick out the CD's that would shuffle in the player for the night—something lively, familiar to the crowd, but not too loud. Most nights we'd play some jazz and a little Big Band Music, throwing in some Roger Whittaker, Roy Orbison and perhaps a little Steve Tyrell or Patsy Cline or Ian Tyson, a cowboy storyteller through music.

At the last minute, everything would be prepared, the house clean and we'd be showered and dressed, ready to greet the guests. I'd walk around the house turning on just the right amount of lighting, as the doorbell rings with our first guest. It's so much fun to greet everyone.

"Hello! Just put your coats or purses on the master bed and come on in."

The music and voices and anticipation of sharing the fruits of our labors carries me away to a heavenly place. I remind everyone that the appetizers are in the kitchen and the bar is in the laundry room.

"Dinner will be served in an hour so please mingle and enjoy. Feel free to wander out to the screen porch or the deck."

Most just pick one place and cram closely in so they can stay together and hear every bit of the storytelling that begins immediately. Someone has been travelling or working on a house project or has news of a family member. We all want to listen. This group has learned how to volley the conversation very well so that no one talks over each other. Everyone takes turns having the floor to share their story. I flit in and around, offering to refill drinks while moving into the kitchen to check all the timing and preparations for our meal.

The women all want to help. Some nights I say, "Thank you, but Oscar and I have this," and he and I act as waiter and waitress all night long. Other nights, when the ladies arrive, I have them each pull a paper out of the hat, which indicates the course for which they will be my designated helper. This way they know when it's their turn to help me serve and they can relax for the rest of the evening.

This particular night Oscar and I were doing the serving. We had the table extended all the way in the small dining room and so once folks were seated, they were packed in like sardines and there was no moving around. Everyone always wants to know where they should sit. I make suggestions or some nights I actually have place cards marking their designated seat. We started the night with a salad from the Rusty Pelican restaurant in Miami, Florida. I love to share the stories of the recipes as I serve, explaining how this recipe found its way to our table from a restaurant or family member. The Rusty Pelican salad is really all about the dressing, which I love because you make it days before the party. Just before serving, you put the lettuce onto the salad plate and ladle on the dressing, filled with shrimp, tomatoes and hard-boiled eggs. I also love to make homemade Green Goddess dressing. There is also the salad we endearingly call Shirley's salad, because she brought it to a potluck one time and we all loved it. To this day I am delighted when my daughter, who does not love entertaining, tells me she has gone to a gathering and brought Shirley's salad.

It is so wonderful to sit around the table and break bread together and share and laugh. As the hostess, my heart is full just to hear someone ask, "Please pass the butter." Sometimes a story is so hysterical I end up with the giggles, such uncontrollable giggles that if I try to talk no one can understand me. "Uh-oh, she has the giggles again," someone declares. I am sure there is no greater medicine than a great big belly-laugh or a fit of uncontrollable giggles. This is worth all the work and preparation.

When all the salad and dinner dishes are stacked into the

kitchen, it's time for coffee and dessert. After-dinner drinks are offered, and there are always a few takers for after-dinner liqueurs like Kahlua, Bailey's or Frangelico, served straight up in a tiny crystal glass for sipping. On this particular night, it was all about the dessert; I made a new recipe gathered on a recent trip to Sedona, where we visited a restaurant recommended for their goat cheese cheesecake. Oscar and I tried it, and after some coaxing, I talked the chef out of the recipe, given to me handwritten on a piece of paper. It requires no topping because it's so rich and delicious just by itself. The music stopped shuffling by now and the table is quiet for just a moment with the anticipation of the first bite into this new recipe. Sounds of ecstasy circle the table. *My heart is full to have these dear friends enjoying our food and fellowship.* For me entertaining is more than a hobby or passion; it is a ministry to bring people together and make a place of peace, comfortable enough for them to be willing to share themselves. I find the combination of art, ministry and hospitality deeply satisfying and fulfilling.

Over the next decade, several couples decided we should try travelling together—RV trips and cruising. Since we all liked to dance, if we were cruising together, we'd walk into a room with an empty dance floor and all of us would get on the floor and fill the room with energy. We'd also have dances at our subdivision clubhouse or go to a local country club for New Year's Eve. In Texas, one can have friends in high places and friends in low places. In our little group, we learned we could go to high places, but we also liked the low places…. the honkytonks. Well, maybe Darlene and I liked the honkytonks more than the others did.

There was a famous honkytonk in Willis called Bob Will's. It was dark, with low ceilings and loud music and walls grungy brown from years of cigarette smoke. Oscar and I loved bellying up to the bar at Bob Will's place. This one time…we decided we should gather up our dancing group, and eight of us went to dance at Bob Will's. When Oscar opened the front door billows of smoke came out and the vibration of the loud music pulsed under our feet. Peeking in, Ron seemed hesitant, his eyes scanning the rough-looking clientele. Leaning into Ron, Oscar smirked and whispered, "Don't worry—they issue us guns with our cover charge." It was untrue, but it was hysterical.

Boy, that was some night. The crowd was certainly entertaining. There were scantily dressed women dancing closely with cowboys in tight blue jeans. Darlene leaned into me and whispered, "They obviously just need to get a room." We worried about nothing but having a good time while we laughed and danced the night away.

We didn't go back there much after that, though. We found a different dive, closer to home, to satisfy the need for a dark, smokey honkytonk night.

This circle of friends would change my life profoundly. I learned so much from them, especially the women. Their friendships gave me strength and confidence, so that I felt more comfortable in my own skin than ever before. I brought Adrienne with me and I was comfortable and liked myself. These warm, inviting, educated, lively, mature women invited me into their hearts, which allowed me to be my authentic self—the good, the bad and the ugly. Their friendship and warmth radiated light into my life and gave me energy. I only hoped I could pay this feeling forward.

My new circle of friends also wanted to teach me about gardening. I did not bring a green thumb with me to Texas. On a visit to see our Willis home, my dear mentor and Big Daddy Tom declared it to be a strong, dependable home and gave us his blessing. He was happy for us. He did say, however, that "a good painting deserves a good frame." Since our house had no landscaping or flower beds, he told us, "Frame your house with beds and learn to garden."

That was such good advice. The house had grass and a lot of trees because we were in the piney woods area of Texas, but it needed garden beds. Tom's wife Bobbie was a great gardener and so were my new friends. They all helped me through a long period of trial and error. We dug out beds around the house. Then we dug them wider. We started planting bushes and succulents, because Oscar always loved the desert. This digging in the dirt was hard, hard work—planting and tending, creating a heaven on earth.

Digging in the dirt was physically challenging but good for my soul. I pushed my body to its limits, so gratified when a plant took root and flourished. Gardening offered me time for contemplation and meditation. Observing the seasons for planting brought me great comfort, because as sure as winter could be hard on the plants, just around the corner would be spring—just as when there is winter in my soul, I can be sure the light of spring is just around the corner.

Gardening—or digging in the dirt, as I call it—also reminds me how things need attention. You need to turn over the dirt or support a leaning stalk. Perhaps it's time to deadhead the flowers. Growing things calls for daily attention. *I need to pay attention to my spiritual and emotional needs on a regular basis, pruning and fertilizing and turning over new ideas and attitudes.* The plants and flowers and dirt provide reminders for me that my body and soul, friends, family and community all need this same attention in order to flourish.

Our street was filled with young neighbors. They would stop and chat whenever they saw us in the yard working or rocking on the front porch. They sent their children down for Mr. Oscar to help fix bikes or share one of his beloved ginger snaps. It didn't take very long for our roots to grow deep, there in the heart of Willis, Texas. We developed deep friendships with shared passions. Oscar had his RV to play with all the time. I was learning to garden and entertain. It was a nice place for the family scattered around the United States to come visit—pull up a chair, play a game, have a chat. We'd take out-of-town visitors to see the USS Texas, the Blue Bell ice cream factory, the Texas prison museum, or horseback riding in Huntsville State Park. We were touched by the friendships and family who were now strongly woven into our lives. I protected the walls of my heart for many years, but here I let my walls down. I was open and I felt free. This underlined my core belief that nobody makes it on their own. Community is an important ingredient to our individual growth and strength. It is vital to touch someone and to be touched, not only physically but in our hearts.

We decided it was time for us to find a church home. Oscar wanted to continue as a Catholic, and I was fine with that, but there was no Catholic church in Willis. We visited a large church in Conroe, 10 miles south of our home, where Oscar's Uncle Bud and Aunt Joann attended. It was OK, but we decided to keep looking. We looked 10 miles north at a 100-year-old parish in New Waverly with a small, beautiful chapel. It was warm and welcoming, and we both fell in love with it the moment we walked in. We became members there and had a place of worship to call our own, further deepening our Texas roots. Now that we were consistent again in our Sunday attendance, our faith journey blossomed. Father Joseph was anxious to make us welcome. Oscar told him he was "not a Catholic in good standing" and I was open about the fact that I wasn't even Catholic. Father Joseph didn't care. We were in church every Sunday, contributing our monthly tithe and engaging with the congregation. That was as Catholic as we needed to be.

One day Father Joseph asked if we would like a blessing for our home, and conducted a deeply personal ceremony for us. The three of us gathered around a picture of Jesus. Father Joseph said prayers and we joined him in the reciting of our Lord's Prayer. He took out the vial of holy water, and we walked together as he sprinkled every room in the house with holy water while we prayed for God's blessing in our home. God was surely listening. Many blessings showered us in that home.

Luella

Shortly after we moved to Willis my mother came to visit. We sat on the back deck under the trees and she whispered, "don't let anyone visit or see this place."

"Why would you say that Mom?"

"Because they will think you won the lotto—it's so nice."

That made me feel so good. My mother and I shared a complicated relationship. Now that I had this wonderful circle of women around me, I was able to appreciate my mother as a woman.

Luella grew up living in the back of her dad's upholstery shop. The family was poor. Baths were in a portable tub in the shop and bath water was shared with the whole family. There were three siblings: Luella, Aaron and Adriana, who suffered from Down's Syndrome and died at age 12. Life wasn't easy. Luella was ambitious though and wanted to go to college. It was unusual for a woman born in 1921 to attend college, especially a poor woman. Luella was determined and creative and she was college-bound.

My story started with Leonard meeting Luella so you know that part of her story. She went on a date, met a guy and they dated only a few times before getting married ten days later. She gave birth to four children and had two miscarriages.

She was a child star's stage mother in Hollywood—one with grace, who folks liked. She was a bookkeeper, working for 3M, Sun Oil Company, retail boutiques, accountants and attorneys. She must have had gypsy in her blood because she was comfortable and energized by the constant moving from apartment to apartment, house to house and coast to coast.

She spoke French and fluent pig-Latin. She was always on a diet. She taught us how to stretch a nickel to a dime. She loved looking at model homes. She taught us you could live without a car. She liked the art of gold and silver leafing on antique furniture. She loved French beading. She taught us how to walk through darkness gracefully as she faithfully walked alongside our father through his four-year battle with cancer.

After he died, she cut her hair in a buzz, packed a backpack and bought a ticket to Europe. It was what a woman at fifty years old, after four years of intense caregiving, needed to do before contemplating the penniless life that lay ahead. Take some time! Breathe. Center one's compass. For six months in 1972 Luella toured Europe, staying in hostels and surviving on French bread and cheese. Her brother had moved to Stockholm about fifteen years earlier to be the headmaster of the prestigious ballet school. She used his studio apartment as a trail head between train rides and touring. It was adventurous for a fifty-year-old woman in 1972 to backpack alone in Europe. Luella was progressive, smart, sassy, well-spoken and very beautiful.

After six months, it was time to go home. She needed to find a job and a place to live, since she sold the condominium she and dad owned, despite his advice to hold on to it for a year after his death.

This one time...she wanted me to go with her for a mother/daughter weekend at a Miami spa that ran a special each year at the end of the season. What a treat it was for me to go for a weekend filled with spa treatments and for mom to have her daughter with her for the whole weekend. We had an adequate room across from the main spa. We took all our "spa" meals in a main dining room, cruise style. Each morning and each afternoon we'd go to the treatment area, disrobe, get wrapped in a sheet and sit on the benches in blissful silence waiting for our masseuse. I ended up with the same masseuse for each and every treatment. I've had a lot of massages in my life and I enjoy the quiet and being carried away into another time and place. This masseuse wanted to talk the entire time and what was so odd is that she had been injured as a young adult and had a permanent tracheotomy, so whenever she talked, she had to hold one hand over her throat. How she managed to give me the best treatments is beyond me. In between massages, Mom and I would fill our time with lounging at the pool, where Mom was proud and delighted to introduce me to the other ladies. I was the only one under 70 I'm sure. That weekend is one of my fondest memories of our time together, just the two of us.

After raising four loving children and burying a husband, Mom seemed OK with a modest, quiet life. I don't believe she thought she'd live to a very old age, but she made it to her 80's. She died without complaint, facing death bravely. It was an honor to help walk her home as a family unit—all four of her children together. I remember the day my brother Terry called to say she had been diagnosed with Leukemia. "She has 2—6 weeks to live," he said. I flew to California right away. We made plans with my brothers, who lived in California near mom, and my sister in Idaho, making sure that Mom was never alone. We also wanted time to be together.

As I reflect back on the last weeks of my mother's life, I feel such tenderness. She was playful. She would say things like, "I think they have the wrong file. I feel fine." Mom wondered why we were paying her so much attention, and didn't seem to understand the gravity of the diagnosis. At one point the doctors suggested she wear pads on her body like a football player, since they were afraid a fall could start a bleeding episode that couldn't be stopped. She yo-yo dieted her entire life and by coincidence when she was diagnosed, she was at a slim, petite size 6. She said, "There is no way I'm wearing those pads, making me look like a size 14."

She was only a social drinker, but when I was there and would pour my nightly cocktail, she would ask, "What are you drinking?"

"I'm having a Scotch, mom."

"I think I should start drinking Scotch. I'll have one of those with you."

She put on a smile and tapped into her sense of humor. Not

wanting us to worry, she told us she had taken care of everything. She made arrangements with the Neptune Society, a prepaid cremation service that was established in the early 1970's. Since she purchased the plan, all we had to do was call the 800 number. She never used foul language until her very last days, when she would jokingly declare daily, "This is the shits!"

At the end, all four of us gathered to be together. We were joined by my sister-in-law Jane, who provided strength, calm and gentleness to our circle. We wanted to be together and to be with our mom. My older brother Terry had been named by my mother to make all her final decisions. Hospice was called in, with the mission of keeping Mom comfortable during her journey to the other side. We rearranged the living room of her one-bedroom apartment so that the hospital bed would fit. At one point I remember all five of us standing around her bed telling stories and talking about daily stuff. Mom was failing and we were keeping her sedated so that she would not be in pain. We didn't think she was awake but as we pondered and spoke aloud about our mother's fate, she chimed in, without opening her eyes, "You know I can hear you."

The doctor had just been there and given us a supply of morphine. Nowadays it is most often administered intravenously through a drip, but they gave us pills of the powerful drug. Mom was so out of it we weren't sure she could swallow it. Somehow the doctor knew that my oldest brother, while looking cleancut at the time, had been a hippie in his former life; he turned to Terry and told him to crush the pills like cocaine or heroin. The only instructions were to "stay ahead of the pain and keep her comfortable." We all looked to Terry for his understanding, empathy and guidance, respecting and honoring whatever he said. We were united in one of the most spiritual, loving experience in my lifetime.

Terry said the medical directive was clear about not administering any water, which might be construed to help prolong her life. No one wanted that—not now. But how would we get that dry morphine pill down her? How could she swallow it without food or water? I reminded everyone that only a few weeks ago she had taken to having an evening Scotch with me. A plan was born and my brother crushed the pill and placed some of the morphine on a spoon, mixing it with a few drops of Scotch. One of us gently lifted her head and asked her to open her mouth. We cried and we laughed. That one-bedroom apartment was prayerful and solemn. It was a sanctuary. I knew we were on holy ground and we found shelter in communion with each other, which brought an inner calm that surpassed all understanding and strengthened our bond.

As I look back at this shared time, it brings pride to my heart to have shared a time when we each had the greater good of someone else as our anchor. Together we shared an energy and spirit that helped our mother walk gently to the other side. We were blessed to be together in such a union, on that unsurpassed journey of love.

Since that time, I have had many losses and many friends who have had losses. My personal experience helps me listen with empathy to each of their journeys. I brag about how my mom was so generous and progressive in her thinking, making her arrangements so that it was easier for us after she died. Death is a realistic part of life. It's not morbid. My friends and I talk openly about death and the end-of-life arrangements we have made, networking ideas for funeral plans like younger folks discuss the latest app for a phone. I believe it is one of the greatest gifts you can give your loved ones to have your legal affairs in order and some arrangements made regarding your end-of-life wishes for your care and death. I urge everyone to not be afraid to openly have that conversation with your family. You can end the conversation by saying you hope this doesn't happen anytime soon and move on to telling a funny story, but don't turn away from the hard discussion. It's such an important and spectacular gift.

Shortly after my mother passed away, a dear friend gave me a tree in her honor. For some time, I left the tree in its pot sitting on my front porch. Rocking on the front porch with my coffee in the morning, I could have a chat with Mom. In the evening with a Scotch, I could talk out my day with her. There's an old camp phrase, if you see the trailer rocking, don't come knocking. Well, several of my neighbors knew that while Mom was there on the porch, if I was sitting there rocking, they should not come knocking, because that was my time with Mom.

Mom's tree flourished and was very happy there on the porch, but on the anniversary of her passing I told her it was time to settle in and establish her roots. We had a little ceremony and planted her in a cozy area beside the house. Here's the thing—I didn't know a lot about trees back then and soon she began to outgrow the spot I picked for her. So I went and had a talk with her.

"Mom," I said, "it seems like your whole life you moved from house to house, apartment to apartment and coast to coast. We always thought it was because Dad was a travelling salesman. Then he died and you kept moving. Well, it seems it's time to move again."

So even in the afterlife, true to her spirit, we dug up Mom's roots and moved her. It was hysterical; we laughed and laughed.

I believe Mom is still laughing and smiling down at me. I talk to her every day. That is particularly comforting to me and significant because of the complicated relationship we shared. She was so busy with my brother's Hollywood career that she didn't really get to raise me. My early childhood was marked by long spaces of solitude. We shared my early teenage years, but mostly at the VA hospital with my dying father, while she was walking a very difficult path of her own. Then I joined the religious cult and Dad died and we both fought our own battles to survive.

As a young woman I didn't understand how she was always looking out for me, loving me unconditionally and trying to reach my soul. She helped me walk again after polio, refusing to accept a disability for her youngest child. She visited me in the sequestered, secluded commune—keeping her eye on me. She provided a home for me and my family when we came out of the commune, helping us get on our feet. She loved me, but I didn't appreciate the depth of her love then.

Now I know. I feel her strength and love and grace. I hear her voice saying, "Young lady, get that hair out of your eyes," or "Save your money, save your money." I hear her voice reminding me, "You take yourself where ever you go." I hear her singing

"Someone's in the Kitchen with Dinah" and saying to me, "Honey, we're OK—you're OK."

I'm sorry Mom for the things I did that hurt you and the things I didn't do that hurt you. I miss you more and more, Mom, and I am proud to be your daughter.

Mom's passing was sad but we were also relieved for her that she did not suffer long. The communion and spiritual connection between my brothers, sister and I is the strongest bond in my life and that would please my mother so very much. We were all keenly aware of the strength instilled in us by both of our parents. That bond would allow us all to carry on. Mom would want us to pack a bag, bring her with us deep in our hearts and continue life.

Continuing Adventures

The prayers, tears, joys and dreams of all past, present and future generations are held in the very dirt of the Earth. When I travel and see the different lands and people, they stir in me a sacred feeling in a timeless realm with a spiritual element that astounds my senses and binds me to those generations. I feel grounded and connected across time to the communities that have been in the same exact place before me and left their energy behind. It moves me deeply, evoking empathy as I try to imagine what their lives were like. I recognize that sometimes people in other cultures have very different customs, yet we are all human beings and fundamentally not all that different one from another.

In so many ways, I feel related to the elements of the earth. The place I stand on reminds me of the very earth from which I am made. When I hear a gentle breeze, I feel related to the air by my own breath and the rise and fall of my chest. The power of the ocean reminds me not only of God's power, but also makes me keenly aware of that power within me. I observe the strength of the trees and yet their ability to bend reminds me of my internal ability to adapt. The landscapes and cultures call to me, urging me closer to communion with human generations, earthly places and God. My heart fills with amazement and gratitude for the opportunity to explore our planet and develop the art of travel.

I need those times on the ocean or on the open road, hiking a new trail or sitting with my feet in the sand. It is a way for me to be still and know God and know myself better. There is a certain wanderlust, a fire burning inside of me, that was fueled by being joined to a soul mate who shares the same desire for adventure. While some research shows that wanderlust is about restlessness and reflects an unsettled spirit, it is also a reflection of someone who loves life deeply and lives it to the extreme. I confirm that both of these are true of myself at different times. Sometimes the restlessness that simmers inside of me causes friction in the way I move in the world, but sometimes it keeps me striving to be better and to do more, filling me with energy to love deeply and to make the effort to live life to the fullest. I recognize that I can be fulfilled right where I am in my own home, but travel is an art that requires me to listen to my internal energy. The artist's challenge, be it cooking, quilting, gardening or travel, has a certain static tension that settles as the treasures beneath the surface are revealed. I find myself compelled to be persistent until the chaotic energy pushing me inside calms down and I find clarity. When I'm in sync with the creativity stirring inside me, I feel my whole body exhale and my spirit calm.

Travel is also a way to connect with family and friends all over the globe. Sometimes the travel is about disconnecting from everything familiar, exploring a totally new place with new people. For me, travel is one of the strategies I use to cope with the hardships of life. Every aspect, from planning to execution, builds resilience. I look back with delight, glad that in my youth, while I was able, I did it. I knew my legs might fail me some day, whether I'd been a polio survivor or not, and so I needed to do these adventures while I could. My explorations of places and people hold special meaning because these experiences changed my heart in many ways.

Channeling the art of exploration, we followed our hearts to Texas, knowing that everything would work out. Once we were rooted and settled, we were humbled by the good fortune coming to us everywhere we looked. The life we were living far exceeded anything we imagined. Oscar and I never made a lot of money, but we lived within our means and that gave us options. Our marriage worked so well because we had open discussions about finances on a regular basis. We were on the same page, sharing a similar relationship to money.

A few years after the move Oscar asked, "Are you sure you want to give up your legal career?" He encouraged me to pursue a job that would make use of my paralegal degree. I found my way to a well-respected law firm close to home. They offered me a full-time position, which presented a problem because I didn't want full-time work. Oscar and I needed time to travel. I didn't want a high-powered, high-paying full-time job, following the career path that most modern professional women at age 50 would want. I wasn't like most women. First of all, I was married to someone 18 years older than me, and at age 68 Oscar was wanting to slow down a bit. Our ages didn't make much of a difference in our daily living, but sometimes in big life choices we had to compromise and meet in the middle. My rejecting a full-time career was part of that balance. When the law firm agreed to my request for a 4-day work week and six weeks a year vacation, I leapt for joy. Through work, I would be able to meet more folks in the community, and there was more discretionary spending money in our budget. We had places to go and people to see.

I like the idea of keeping my career current, but no amount of money can replace free time. I'm not like most women who feel they have to be able to do it all. I'm lucky to have the choice of whether to stay home or be in the work force; I remember when I had no choice but to work to eat. Now, I don't feel pressure to prove anything. I work to make money for things I love to do, like travelling. I don't care about a huge house or luxury cars. Oscar and I design our lives weaving in travel as part of our natural flow, as necessary to us as water and air are to life.

There is a difference between visiting and vacation, but occasionally we would combine the two. Our children were having children, so we began to plan trips and visits with our grandchildren. There were so many precious moments. This one time...a daughter called to say her children wanted to be with us for Christmas.

"That's wonderful. When do ya'll want to come?" I asked.

"No, you don't understand. They want to come by themselves."

Santa was coming to our house! Christmas Eve, as I tucked sweet Ariel into bed, reminding her that we had to get some sleep because Santa was coming, she held up a piece of paper and said, "Grandma, can you please give this to Santa?"

"What is that?"

"Well, I thought maybe I asked Santa for too much so I wrote a letter changing what I want."

My heart was so touched, because this sweet little child deserved the world. I knew for a fact she hadn't asked for too much. I talked fast, saying, "Santa already left the North Pole so he won't be able to get this new letter, sweetheart, but I'm sure he got your first letter and you have nothing to worry about. You get some sleep."

It was a perfect Christmas with hearts full of love and plenty of gifts, especially the generous gift that our daughter gave in allowing us to have alone time with the children. Those two stole our hearts from the moment they were born—such tender, sweet, loving, respectful children.

Of course, each of the grandchildren touched us in different ways. Over the years we tried to plan special trips for each set of grandchildren, not only to have the pleasure of spending time with them, but also expose them to our passion for travel and have them see other places and broaden their horizons. One set we took on a three-night Looney Tunes themed-cruise out of Orlando. Another set we took on a six-week camping trip from Florida all the way to Colorado and New Mexico to see Mesa Verde National Park. Six weeks was a long time. On a short visit it's easier to keep your best foot forward, but on a longer sojourn your guards come down, which made the visits more honest and real. They saw a lot of the country and we all saw each other at our best and our worst. It's part of every day and the closeness of travel and the unexpected situations, but hopefully by seeing us vulnerable and spent, we made bonds we would not have forged otherwise.

Our friends were always surprised by how long we would plan the visits with our grandchildren. This one time...we had four of them, two sets of cousins, fly from Atlanta to Texas for a three-week visit. The youngest was maybe five and the oldest was nine. I prepared for their arrival with a trip to the hobby store. I was going to be working the first two weeks of their visit, so Papa would have the kids during the day on his own. Every day was like arts and crafts camp, with models to assemble and paint-by-number kits to do. We bought used bikes so that each of them had a bike to ride while they were visiting. The subdivision was gated, so we felt safe letting them ride off on their own and they loved being independent and acting so grown up. The oldest was put in charge of the group and would wear a watch so they could be sure to be back by a certain time. Papa taught them how to fix bikes, use a soldering gun and perform maintenance on the RV. The kids loved helping Papa go to the ranch where he volunteered helping abandoned and abused horses, even when it meant all they were going to do was shovel poop! When I'd get home from work, we'd have dinner and then there was more game-playing and riding bikes and swimming and TV. It was marvelous having so much uninterrupted quality time with them.

The last week of our visit together was an RV trip to take them home. We had a brand new 23' class C Tioga motorhome with a couch that flipped out to make a very uncomfortable full-size bed for us. The children slept either in the queen-size bed over the cab of the truck, or on the dining table, which converted to a bed. Frankly, I don't know how we all fit in that thing. We had a few mishaps, like the engine problem on the first day, somewhere in Mississippi. We spent 7 hours in a coffee shop waiting while the mechanic fixed our RV. He put us ahead of everyone else in the shop, seeing us stranded with those 4 kids. They were good as pie, coloring and playing, and by the day's end we were back on our way, but we got to camp that first night already worn out.

"What are we having for dinner tonight Grandma?"

Oh my gosh... dinner tonight. "You know, we have some fresh milk and a big bag of Oreo cookies. How about cookies and milk for a camp dinner tonight?"

After three weeks with the kids and a day in the repair shop, I was too pooped to participate. Even though they were easy, good children—this was a lot. I might have been the coolest grandma ever that night as we sat and ate cookies and milk for dinner. Then the kids were getting ready for bed and the oldest said, "Grandma, my underwear is in the suitcase in the car."

"We are not going back out to the car for anything. We all need to just get ready for sleep."

"But I always put my clean underwear on at night."

I hesitated; then I said, "Just turn them inside out."

In one evening, I went from the coolest grandma to the craziest grandma ever!

The time and money and effort to plan that trip was so worth it. We loved every minute and the precious time was priceless.

As we opened our hearts to say yes to every opportunity to connect with friends and family through travel, opportunities and ideas kept knocking on our door. We used travel and adventure to center ourselves, bringing joy and light into our souls—and as a byproduct it radiated out a shining light that created a ministry of sorts. I feel like this is somewhat of a ministry for me to share my stories and experiences with my neighbors, friends and family. When I share, then they share and it opens our hearts to connect. We connect with each other and share our insights and observations.

Some of our trips were inspired by history. On a trip to Hawaii, just the two of us, we visited the USS Arizona and communed with the souls who lost their lives there. By RV we visited the Civil War battlefields in Virginia, listening in horror to reenactments of the hand-to-hand combat that took place on our own soil, feeling bound to those men and their families. Entering a church near Quebec City I was deeply moved by the crutches adorning the walls. Generations of disabled folks visited, abandoning their crutches in the strong faith that they had been healed by their journey to that sanctuary. Once we visited Germany, and my spirit felt anxious and uncomfortable being in the country that had supported Hitler. It was a type of time travel, experiencing the past, present and future converging in my body and soul.

One of the best RV trips we ever took was visiting Albuquerque, New Mexico for the annual balloon festival. We made campground reservations a year in advance, because any kind of lodging for that week is booked up and at a premium. We had to race the clock to drive out there in time to set up camp before the opening balloon launches. When we arrived, there was a mix-up with our reservation; they tried to put us in a car parking space instead of the full campsite we reserved. When we said that was unacceptable, the owner said sarcastically, "Well—try and find another place to stay in the city now."

That's exactly what we did. We called around and a few sites said, "You shouldn't be treated that way. We have no room but come on over and we'll find you a spot to dry camp." The idea of a week of dry camping wasn't wonderful because we wanted water and electric hook-ups, but we preferred that to staying in a parking space for which they were charging us premium rates with a bad attitude to boot.

Once we were settled, we had the experience of a lifetime. The first morning, we rose at 3 a.m. to be at the launch field by 5 a.m. The field was covered by 300 flat balloons on the ground, waiting to be inflated. Whoosh. Whoosh. Whoosh. As each colorful balloon filled with air, it slowly began to stand straight above the basket. Marvelous shapes and colors filled the field. We ran from basket to basket, helping the crews by holding a rope until it was their time to launch. It was so exhilarating to watch 300 balloons ascend into the sky. To this day, when I remember that event, I can feel the energy of the day coursing through me.

We loved travelling in the RV, but we were just as at home on the sea. Oscar was still working as a ship surveyor and we took many cruises to Mexico and the Caribbean. We were often invited to sit at the captain's table. This one time...at the end of the meal the captain turned to me and asked, "Is there anything I can do for you?"

"Yes, I would love a visit to the bridge," I answered.

"I'm sure I can make those arrangements," the captain answered.

I quickly added that we were travelling as a group of 10 and asked if we could all go on the bridge. His eyes got big and he seemed a little stunned, but he said he'd try.

When we finished dinner with the captain, we ran to join our friends, who were finishing dessert at our regular dining table. We were so excited to tell them that we were getting a private tour of the bridge! It was a great opportunity, and I was pleased with myself for being so bold.

Another time, we took our third cruise through the Panama Canal. Oscar was working that trip and so the crew all knew who he was. I think the canal passage can be tedious because it takes several days to pass through the canals, listening on the loud speakers to the engineering facts and details about the locks. This time, however, the captain invited Oscar and me to join him for a day on the bridge during the passage. I knew I needed to be as quiet as a church mouse while staying as close to Oscar as his shadow. We spent the day moving quietly from one side of the bridge to the other, observing how narrow the clearance was on either side of the ship. It was remarkable.

As we approached the end of the last lock, the engines revved up so that we could quickly get out of the locks and give clear passage to the ship coming straight at us. That was the moment when the Panama pilots who were on board had to jump off. You heard me. They had to jump from the ship to their pilot boat. That day there was a trainee who froze and didn't want to jump. The captain was livid because he had to slow down for the trainee who refused to jump.

The quiet bridge changed abruptly when the captain shouted, "I can't slow anymore. If he doesn't jump in the next 60 seconds, push him!"

Two minutes later, we were at high speed getting out of the way of the oncoming traffic. I have no idea if the pilot jumped or was pushed. Either way I knew how lucky I was to be a fly on the wall in all these different circumstances and to think about what others go through in their jobs—from the pilot trainee to the captain. For sure they all had a story to tell their families that night.

Another time, Oscar was about to attend one of his chemical ships for an inspection at Houston. The weather wasn't very good, so the seas were pretty rough. The night before he told me that he was a little scared.

"Why?" I asked.

"Sometimes when I call on a ship," he explained, "I have to board a pilot boat that takes me out to the ship at anchor. I strap my gear on my back and stand on the edge of the pilot boat while it bobs up and down in the rough waters waiting for the right time to jump to the rope ladder hanging down the side of the ship." Timing the jump from the boat to the ship required precise reflexes. I shouldn't have laughed but the vision of Wiley Coyote splat on the side of the ship was all I could envision.

The last several ships he attended, a crew member would say, "Commander, let me carry your gear for you."

We both agreed it was time for him to stop climbing rope ladders. He could continue to survey his ships, but only if there was a gangway available to walk aboard.

It was always important to us to have a trip planned on the calendar, giving us something to look forward to with excitement. Our 25th wedding anniversary was a great reason to celebrate and some of our dearest friends joined us on a Greek island cruise. The pristine beaches and rich blue waters were breathtaking. The most amazing day of that cruise was in Santorini, when we took a tour to see a volcano. I didn't realize it meant we were to climb to the top of a volcano. My legs were not strong and I was walking with a cane everywhere by that time, but my friends as well as everyone on the tour were so patient with me, encouraging me and chanting—you can do it! I thought about the eleven doctors who said I'd never walk again; I thought of my mother who refused to believe it. Once again, on a journey in a land far away, I was reminded of how life should be every day, as we cheer each other on to victory. Up at the top, I breathed in the crisp clear air and felt my heart overflowing with accomplishment and friendship. This is what travel is all about for me—it's why I spend hours dreaming, planning and executing this passion of mine.

Back home, ready for the next adventure, the phone rang and it was Jaak Rannik, an old shipmate of Oscar's. He owned a home at a resort in the Dominican Republic.

"Please join me here in the DR with Thad and Norm and their wives for a reunion of sorts," he said.

"Of course, just tell us when and where and we'll be there!" we replied.

There were so many good things about that trip. The best thing was hearing those men share stories of their service time together. They laughed and hugged and shared an indescribable bond. One night we sat basking in the sweet air and warmth of the fellowship, listening to the faint sound of the ocean with the glass doors open, as Jaak opened a very fine bottle of Scotch. Jimmy Buffet was playing on the stereo, and Oscar took my hand and we danced for a euphoric moment; it was magical to be in his arms swaying to the music with his dear shipmates nearby. Saying yes to life, I felt completely and totally satisfied.

On another trip, we decided to do a small ship river cruise, which was something we had never done before. Oscar's family came from Belgium, and I had family from Amsterdam, so we focused on that region of the world. I wanted to stand in Holland and see the fields of tulips. We researched the cities and itineraries, focusing our attention on Antwerp, the city from which Oscar's dad sailed when he was twelve to come to America. Oscar's Pa travelled half way across the world to a better life. We were now crossing back to that very place, and looked forward to visiting the museum in Antwerp dedicated to the immigrants who left their homeland behind for a new life.

We were surprised to find a large, elaborate museum focusing on the emigrants who sailed on the Red Star Line. There were pictures of emigrants and you could pick up a phone and listen to that person's story as to why they wanted to leave, and what their hopes for a new life had been. Most left because of poverty and looked forward to the opportunities America would bring.

In the first room there was a massive tube replicating where the passengers had to put all of their luggage so that it could be steamed and decontaminated. We moved through the museum at the same time as a local group of nine-year-old Belgian students, who were also listening to the passengers' stories. We reverently and silently passed the listening devices between us.

In the last room there was a movie playing. The children all went in and sat down. A few minutes later we decided to join them and I sat down on the one remaining seat on the bench in the last row while Oscar stood behind me. The film depicted the journey of the emigrants and showed a film of the straw bags and luggage being put into the sterilization chamber. What we saw next was shocking. The emigrants—men, woman and children—lined up in a very large room, arm's length apart, all facing forward, and disrobed. Sprinklers began to rain disinfectant on them as they stood in place still and naked for quite some time. Amazingly, the children watching the movie did not budge or giggle or make a noise. They watched this part of history with deep respect.

Profoundly moved, I reflected on how connected we were to the generations who had been willing to risk everything for a better life. We were connected to the young ones watching with us as well as to Pa and the legacy of his journey. Later we found his name, Oscar Frank Poppe, Sr. on the manifest in the museum computer. Once again, I was changed by seeing something with my own eyes at a particular moment in time. This was why I had to keep my passion for travel alive...to plan on—to dream on—to move on!

When I look back at the thirty years of RV travel that Oscar and I shared it brings me great joy and many wonderful memories. Sometimes we were just the two of us and sometimes we crammed as many as we could in such a small space but no one seemed to mind, because all that mattered was being together. There were also tough moments, with exhaustion putting us on edge. There was plenty of sunshine but also nail-biting drives on dangerous winding roads or in the pouring rain. You don't make the choice to enter the RV lifestyle because it's a cheaper way to travel. By the time you purchase and maintain your unit and pay for the gas, it can be very expensive. When we started in

1985 a campsite was cheap, but by the year 2013, when we sold our last RV, the campsite rates were pretty high. It's an annual travel budget investment that is quite a commitment, but it has marvelous return.

The world of cruising is also a marvelous way to travel, allowing one to feel the ocean perhaps as a quiet place of solitude or with friends or family in a party atmosphere. We loved travelling with friends. It is a rare treasure to find friends who share the same passion and move to the same rhythm. Sometimes I say that my husband has salt in his blood and I am so happy that when we married, we committed to each other that we would always find a way to be on the ocean. I pinch myself that this girl who at one time didn't have enough to eat or enough money to heat my home, has cruised to see with my own eyes so many places, including the San Blas Islands, the Bahamas, Puerto Rico, Jamaica, Bermuda, the Dominican Republic, the Caribbean Islands, Santorini, Mykonos, Athens, Turkey, Rome, Mexico, Costa Rica, the Netherlands, Italy, Astoria and Victoria. It's the beauty of the people and the places that call to me; seeing these places gives me vision and makes me feel alive. I am beyond grateful to have seen so many places and to have gotten to know so many people.

Life's journey has not been without pain and difficulties but my strategy and solution has been to use travel as a tool bringing me joy and peace and light. It was a choice to sacrifice other things so that we didn't have to put off travel until our retirement years. Now that we are both older and I know how much harder the long days of driving or flying or the miles of hiking would be, I am more pleased than ever to have followed the yearning for travel for all these years.

As I write this, our world is under the threat of the COVID pandemic and all of us feel closed in. It's very claustrophobic not to be able to get on a plane or a ship. My passion for travel has been sustained during COVID by my memories of years gone by. It's a daily challenge to keep hope alive, but I do. I hope that one day I will again feel safe to visit old and new places and continue a life of exploration in which I can behold the beautiful canyons, valleys, rivers and oceans of our majestic Earth and be linked by quiet contemplation to the breath of past and future generations.

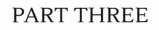

PART THREE

Friends with the Dark

Energy is essential to all living things. I am no student of science, but I know, for example, that two sources of energy are solar and wind. We need to each ask ourselves, how do we use energy? Are we efficient and conservative? What consequences will our choices make? We can think of energy in environmental ways, but I mostly think about the energy within my body that gives me the ability to work, create and socialize. It seems like I can actually feel the atoms and molecules moving inside me.

Energy is a funny thing. A therapist told me once that an extrovert derives energy from other people, while an introvert is depleted of energy by other people. My understanding is that all people can act in an extroverted manner at times, but the proof of one's core identity comes in how much energy you have after interacting with people. I was physically active and engaged in my community, loving the people, places and activities in my life, but I sensed I was depleting my store of energy quickly.

I can create more energy for my life by eating right, taking care of my body, and doing the things I love to do. Flowing water can create energy for the planet. I know my body is made up of 60% water and it's crazy but I can feel my relation to the water. When I hear the sound of water, I feel a vibration resonating within my very core. Water has always played an important role in my personal journey. As a toddler I spent many hours in a pool for therapy as part of my polio recovery. Both the Pacific and Atlantic oceans were the backdrop of my childhood. Marrying a sailor and having the sea become an intimate part of my life was the most natural thing in the world to me.

My life often resembles a gentle flowing river, but sometimes the river begins to rush along with wild strength and power. The water sings a melody to me, begging my body to listen and perhaps sway to the rhythm. The force of gravity moves the river downhill in an ever-changing path. When you step up close along the river's edge, sometimes it's clear all the way to the bottom, revealing beauty below. Sometimes though the river is so wide or muddy that it's difficult to see anything below the surface. When I peer beneath the surface of that beautiful river flowing inside me, I see ever-shifting sand and rock, which has been broken over time.

It was absolutely amazing how well our move to Texas worked out. By the grace of God, hard work and a lot of luck, combined with the willingness to takes risks and be vulnerable, we were living a charmed life. Yet somehow, like the sediment at the bottom of the river, I felt a bit of turbulence stirring in my soul. The curves and rapids of the river were not always easy to navigate and I could feel my energetic balance disturbed. I carried a lot of shame with me and I doubted myself anytime things went amiss. A battle in my mind would ensue as I contemplated my words and intentions, along with others' motives, actions and conversations. *Did I say something wrong? What did I do? What did they mean? Maybe it was nothing? Should I ask? Should I stay silent or should I speak up?*

I tried to trust my sense of intuition. There were many incidents in my life when I knew something was off, but other times I felt my thoughts were irrational and untrue—which did not make them any less disturbing to me. The self-doubt could be overwhelming and I would be so angry with myself because the inner dialogue and conflict drained my energy. It was difficult to still the wild thoughts unleashed in my mind like the raging waters of a flood. I tried to focus on being centered, reminding myself that everything was OK. *I feel deeply immersed in distress. Something is wrong or something terrible is going to happen. What is this dread that*

I feel? I must find a way to stay centered. Why should I feel guilt and shame? Why does the loss and pain of my past revisit me, when I just want to fully appreciate the joy and love surrounding me? Stop reliving the trauma of the past. Get a grip, Adrienne. I need to learn to forgive myself so that I can be healed.

Life was beautiful and lyrical and filled with love and I should have had everything settled in my soul. My self-doubt and uncertainty persisted, though. Being kind to myself wasn't a natural way of being and I did a lot of unproductive dwelling on things I couldn't control. Sometimes I could calm the anxious voices by reminding myself to take it one day at a time. I knew I had to just put one foot in front of the other and move forward, embracing the marvelous experiences and wonderful blessings I was living. I pushed myself to be physically and socially active. Being surrounded by a loving circle of women and family helped me deal with my inner anxiety and fear and provided evidence that my glass was half full, not half empty. Along with the excitement of our travelling adventures, I focused on filling my life with activity and people who reminded me that I was loved. *I am rich with such deep, loving relationships in my life. Why do I still have so much trouble trusting there is truth in these relationships and that I am loved and liked?*

There were many joyous family events to celebrate as our blended family matured. The family was geographically spread out and that made it more important for us to use graduations, birthdays and weddings as ways to stay connected. We attended as many events as possible. I wanted to share and participate and stay alert for situations that might require my help. Not living in the same city with someone meant details might get lost or ignored or hidden in a closet. I remember a time I had to help a young woman escape an abusive husband, when all the others around her only asked her what had she done wrong. I had firsthand experience with dark secrets. I had a few myself. I wasn't trying to be nosey, but I wanted to be available to help if need be. I would want someone to do the same for me. I needed to hone in and sharpen my intuition skills and learn to listen and trust the spirit inside of me. *Pay attention Adrienne Melanie.* It is my duty and honor to listen to those in my circle and discern when to respect their privacy or when they need help and intervention.

We celebrated with one daughter at her online wedding in Vegas, led by an Elvis impersonator. We celebrated with another daughter who earned her college degree after returning to study in her thirties. We celebrated Oscar's dad turning 90 and traveled to Florida for a family reunion. Oscar's oldest son had not been lucky in love until he met Janet, and we were thrilled to join that wedding celebration. One daughter was renewing her wedding vows for their tenth wedding anniversary with a Disney theme celebration and wanted her dad to walk her down the stairs. Overflowing joy filled our lives as our blended family grew with lots of parties and celebrating and kisses and hugs. Naturally there were difficult times too but I just tried to keep my eyes on the horizon.

One of life's dreams and the reason for our move to Texas was to connect on a deeper level with my two children. Perhaps our bonds would be different than other mothers and children because of the different circumstances of their childhood. I looked for places and times and openings that would create connections. It was OK for our relationships to be different. I wanted us to mature together accepting our history as only our beginning, because now it was about sharing who we each had become. I just wanted to be included in their lives and hearts.

There was a big event just around the corner. Oscar was turning 70 and we were going to celebrate in style. I put the word out that we were going on a cruise and hoped friends and family could join us. They did; twenty of us departed Galveston on a Royal Caribbean Cruise Line ship. A wonderful time was had by all. We went to the beach and swam in the glorious ocean and spent a day in Key West doing a pub crawl of our own making. There was a night or two with everyone dressed to the nines in tuxedos and long formals and some of us even spent a little time in the cigar lounge. There was dancing, always dancing, and laughing as I flitted from group to group basking in the joy of this time. I was alive in the moment, filled with gratitude, joy and positive energy.

I looked forward to spring just around the corner, aware that summer would naturally follow, but unaware of the storms that this summer would bring.

In the spring, I began the glorious and gratifying gardening that called to me and enriched my soul. I noticed my legs feeling very heavy, with a burning sensation—a tingling as if the very molecules were on fire. It felt different than just the usual soreness from a day of physical activity. I was glad we had scheduled the initial visit to the polio clinic in Houston at the Texas Rehabilitation Center.

For many years after my paralyzing polio and recovery, I lived free of fear and worry about my polio. I had recovered. As a young adult, I began to push myself more, feeling strong and able-bodied. It was amazing and exhilarating to participate and feel my body functioning fully. Then in 1986 my mother read a newspaper article that shook her to the core. That old fear raised its head. It reported that some 15-40 years after the initial onset of polio, some people who had recovered from paralytic polio were experiencing a disorder showing symptoms of severe fatigue and muscle pain, weakness and atrophy.

It was called PPS, post-polio syndrome. The theory is that a case of polio severe enough to cause paralysis probably destroyed anywhere from 40-60% of the motor neurons, leaving the remaining neurons to do all the work. Motor neurons carry impulses from the brain and spinal cord to the muscles. After years of overuse, the remaining neurons began to break down. One news article talked about FDR and his polio. He built a therapy center at Warm Springs, Georgia. When I made a journey there, I found out that all around the United States there are support groups for polio survivors. It isn't understood why, but apparently PPS attacks women more than men, and the more severe your initial polio, the more chance of PPS. We had cause for concern.

Over the next ten years, although bouts of severe fatigue and muscle weakness would overwhelm me, it still didn't occur to me to connect it to polio. I had a busy career, family, travel and commitments that made me weak and tired. That's all it seemed to be. That's all I hoped it was.

In 2000, when we moved to Texas, I began seeing articles about PPS in the Houston newspaper, and we contacted a local PPS support group, just to be in touch. I continued to experience episodes of fatigue, weakness and numbness, but they would only last a few weeks and then be followed by strong plateaus, sometimes for a year. I was still in denial.

Then in 2006 I found a doctor in Houston who worked with polio patients at the Texas Institute for Rehabilitation. As there were very few doctors left who actually treated polio patients, I decided to visit him for a baseline exam. He talked with me, watched me walk, examined my reflexes and measured my strength levels. I had diminished strength and weakened reflexes. I was unaware of the extent of the damage that had been caused by the virus. As far as he was concerned, there was no doubt—I had Post-Polio Syndrome. He told me that I needed to stop my denial and come to grips with reality.

There is no treatment for PPS other than lifestyle changes. His advice was to throw out the rule of no pain, no gain, and instead adopt the motto "conserve the reserve." The doctor told me I needed to modify my lifestyle and listen to my body. He suggested I begin to use a cane all of the time because it would help me conserve energy. *I can do this.* I found a wooden cane with a comfortable handle at a garage sale, and we, the cane and I, made friends. I was issued a scooter, because at that time I was having difficulty walking for any length of time. I never made friends with the scooter. I used it sometimes at a festival or rodeo or fair, but not in my regular daily life. *I feel weakness and pain. I know I feel tired, but can I feel the actual molecules, atoms and neurons? Surely not, but I am trying to hear what this doctor is saying.*

For me, it was very difficult to adopt a creed of not overdoing, when the experience of "you can do it" had been engrained in the fabric of my soul. Polio survivors are just that—survivors. I learned to be strong and overcome; never to show the world my weakness. I trained myself not to give in to the disability. But now I had to learn to admit to myself: I am disabled. I have Post-Polio Syndrome. There are days when my legs hurt to the bone, when my arm is numb and weak and I am so tired I can't think. Every ounce of energy I have gets used up just in performing daily functions.

Every day brings new anxiety, as I face the question of what the future will hold. The past gives me the courage to face whatever hardships come with hope. I am learning to save energy and strength—like saving money in a bank for a rainy day. It's not always easy because when I feel strong, physically and mentally, I hear the old voices urging me to overcome—push on—don't give in. They haunt and tease me. I'm not sure if they are good or evil—are they voices of courage or destruction? Day by day I try to pay attention, to listen and discern. Sometimes it's right to move forward. Sometimes I need to be still.

In my personal journey with post-polio syndrome, there are still many days of denial. Why, I don't know. It's still so hard to admit I just can't do some things. One day at a time, I try to learn to accept myself for everything I can do and everything I can't. I am grateful for the inner strength my experiences with polio wrought in me. I draw confidence from the knowledge that I am a survivor. I can adapt. I can cope. I can manage my life. I can handle anything. I am proud of myself. I am alive and living life to the fullest with an awareness that life is not a sprint but a marathon so I should pace myself. I am grateful for the courage and determination of my parents. I am grateful for all the years of strength and freedom of movement. I am grateful for the sensitivity of my husband in his awareness of my weaknesses. *God, thank you. Mom, I wish you were here to walk this part of the journey with me. Never give up. Adrienne. Never give up!*

Oscar was very caring and considerate of the lifestyle changes we needed to make. He was also very quiet and withdrawn. We both seemed to be on edge with each other, which was not our normal way of interacting, especially in times of trouble. We were usually very gracious with each other. *I worry that he is worried about me. What is going on in that head of his?* As the heat of the Texas summer rose, the conversations between me and Oscar heated up also. His silence was loud and when he did speak, he seemed angry most of the time. Usually when he's angry, he doesn't shout, but he gets moody. He was on a fairly short fuse and I just didn't understand.

I tried to coax him to talk about it.

"Darling, what's going on?"

"Nothing, I'm fine."

Without making eye contact, he always replied he was fine. He didn't want to talk about anything; he just wanted to be left alone.

Something was definitely wrong. He was so good at hiding it from everyone else in our world that when I asked one of the children or a close friend if they noticed anything wrong, everyone said no. I began to doubt my intuition again. I wondered what I had done; why was he angry with me? *I know I sense something. I'm sure I'm upsetting him, I cannot let go of this need to uncover what is brewing inside of him. What is my intuition telling me?*

The light in his eyes was dim. It was summer outside but it felt as cold as winter in our house. We had good days and bad, like most folks, but the bad days were multiplying. When we argued I felt totally despondent, losing the ability to function. I felt all alone, wondering where the man inside of my husband had gone. *Where are you, God?* I hoped and prayed this was just a phase we were going through.

A few times a month Oscar would pick me up at work for a lunch date. This one particular August day we went to our favorite Chinese place, which was always packed with lunch patrons. They recognized us and sat us down and we ordered our usual lunch specials with heaping amounts of sweet and sour something, the almond chicken or Egg Foo Yung. It was a bit loud, so it was hard to carry on a conversation. I don't remember what we were talking about but when we finished and got in the truck for him to take me back to the office, we picked up the conversation. As we pulled into the parking lot of my office building, the tension grew. We were both upset, but he seemed really angry.

I could have let it go, but I pressed. I don't remember exactly what we were talking about or what I said, but I clearly remember that Oscar responded by shouting, "Why the hell would I care about that when I have cancer?"

"What did you say?"

He repeated himself.

"Oscar, please look at me. What are you saying?"

He told me that eight months earlier he had been diagnosed with aggressive prostate cancer. He had been told that if he did nothing about it, he'd have one year to live. Not wanting to treat it, he kept it a secret.

I was stricken with incredible sadness that he would not trust me enough to know that he could tell me anything. He was the love of my life; we were unstoppable together and could handle anything.

Crying, I asked, "Why didn't you tell me?" The cancer I could deal with, but because of my past, I can't stand secrets.

I kept insisting, "I love you, Oscar. Please, we can handle this. We need to find out about the treatment options. Please stay with me."

I begged him to choose life—to have the will to fight the cancer and live for us—for our family and for our future. I made an appointment with the doctor so I could hear for myself the diagnosis and the options. We drove to Dallas to have a family meeting with my children, now adults, who wanted to remind their Pops just how much he was loved and needed. There are different types of prostate cancer; some types are more aggressive than others. It depends on the Gleason score and at what rate that number increases. Oscar had gone from 1 to 7 in a very short period of time, reflecting an aggressive cancer. The clock was also ticking because Oscar was 70 years old. The doctor said that if he chose radiation or chemotherapy first and it was unsuccessful, he might be too old to qualify for surgery to remove the prostrate. At that time removing the prostate was considered major surgery, with a long recovery and possible side effects that could be life-altering.

Finally, Oscar consented to the surgery. There was a one-year recovery time to allow the body to regain strength. Oscar was a very good patient, always grateful for any assistance given him and never wanting to bother anyone. I felt so very grateful and honored to be the one to help him walk this journey. His body began to heal, but it took time. He had to give up his work with abandoned and abused horses, which he missed greatly, and his other passion of maintaining his RV fell by the wayside, as that required strength and physical stamina. Six months after the surgery he was invited to join a friend on a trip to hike down the Grand Canyon, which he had to decline. The side effect warnings loomed in the background, as we waited the year to see how his body would mend. We were thrilled that the surgery had been successful; they removed all the cancer and somehow, miraculously, the anger in our house had also been replaced with grace and gentleness. Having had the courage to be honest and open with each other made it easier to deal with fears as we tried to cultivate our hopes.

Unfortunately, side effects manifested, forcing Oscar to deal with other issues. I saw this as another opportunity for us to overcome the obstacles put in our way, but this was not just a physical obstacle. His condition began to erode our emotional wellbeing and the social community we had built, as Oscar withdrew, not wanting to participate any longer. Between my new disability affecting my stamina and his compromised body, we were drowning. I was not equipped to help him with all the emotional repercussions of this situation. The doctor said to be patient and give his body time to fully recover. Time passed but his body did not recover. He was in his own world and I was in my own world, each of us battling demons by ourselves.

The church we had been attending never noticed that we were gone. It had been months since we had been to church but no one called to check on us. We turned down social invitations. I was afraid, as my intuition sensed that even though the tension was gone and we shared a certain gentleness now, indifference was creeping in. Oscar was very unhappy that his body had failed him. I didn't tell anyone the details of Oscar's recovery, or lack thereof. A few members of the family seemed almost angry with us that we were not more joyful—after all, the cancer surgery had been successful. I heard frustration in their tones when they told me I should be happy because the cancer was gone and also because I was still walking—so what if I had to use a cane? I was grateful, but that didn't mean I was joyful. Our emotions don't always follow logic. I was unable to explain what was going on under the surface, behind our closed doors and in my mind. They didn't understand that an eclipse had moved over our house and darkness was overcoming the light.

Frustrated with our dark moods and perhaps feeling like they didn't know how to help, some of our family members stepped back from our lives. At least that's how I interpreted it. I was ashamed and angry at myself that I could not summon the joy they wanted to see and I was also disappointed to realize that others don't really want to be around a sad soul. They want the woman who laughs and dances, not the lady singing the blues. *Why should I be ashamed that I am suffering?*

Then one day, the sun was shining and music was playing on the radio as I headed north on my way home from work. In the past I might have had the sunroof open and the volume turned up on the radio to bebop for the drive. This one time...however, my thoughts were loud, drowning out the music, like a massive thunderstorm rolling across the ocean. I could hear it getting closer; I felt it shaking the center of my soul. The sad thoughts were winning. I didn't know if what I was thinking was true or imaginary, but trying to figure it out left me feeling hopeless. *Now I have another secret to keep. No one must know about this battle of incredible sadness and darkness that fills my thoughts.* I was sobbing uncontrollably as I drove down the road. In that moment I realized that I wanted to make my car swerve head on into the oncoming traffic. *No, stop—maybe it would be better to go to some faraway place where no one would find me and just jump off the cliff into the sharp rocks in the water below. What if I don't die? That would be worse for me, for my family and those I will hurt. Let go of this death grip on the wheel, Adrienne. Where are you, God?*

The good and bad thoughts were at war, raging inside of me. I'm not saying I hear literal voices. Some of the battle is residual, from the messages I heard during the commune years: the reels that run in my head reminding me that I am worthless and terrible. Sometimes I feel strong and mature and can reason away the negative messages. Some days they take me by surprise. I think there is light at the end of the tunnel, and then I realize that the light is really a train headed straight for me. Sometimes I am quite melancholy, which isn't always bad because it channels empathy welling up inside of me. However, sometimes it leads me down a path where I feel terribly sad, worthless, a failure and full of shame, drowning in hopelessness. I am lost in a dark cavern full of fear, impossible to navigate. Meanwhile, there is another side of me that is trying to remember the kind, good things about myself that others tell me they see in me so I can believe those things and find reason for hope...reason to live. *My life is not my own to throw away. I must overcome.*

What must it take for someone to take their own life? "How could they? It's so horrible. It's selfish!" Those are the questions and comments I hear made about suicide. I know that a person must be in a lot of pain to see it as their only choice. Sometimes my own pain goes so deep that I consider making the choice to commit suicide. *How many pills and what kind would I have to take? Wouldn't that be the kindest way to go? How long until someone would discover they couldn't get ahold of me?*

One crack in the dam can release the river rapids, flooding my mind. The thoughts and emotions tumble and rush over the broken rocks of my soul. Fortunately, the older I get, the less I struggle. My mature self knows I am blessed and safe. Thank goodness. Nevertheless, I still have those mind battles, when the voices rage and are difficult to calm. I read once that toxic shame is a neurotic irrational feeling of worthlessness, humiliation and self-loathing; a paralyzing feeling that has been inflicted onto an individual through repeated traumatic experiences often, but not always, rooted in childhood. I was not abused or abandoned, unless being in quarantine with polio for six weeks left me with a deep feeling of abandonment. I didn't grow up under terrible circum-stances, unless being lonely is terrible or my experience with the cult would count. Circumstances beyond our control just happen sometimes, but I do blame myself for losing my children and that is a deep grief that rises to the surface regularly. I know I did what I had to do and that I was manipulated while I still had no voice, and thank goodness my children voice their approval and love, but sometimes I still wonder about the what-ifs of different choices. I reflect back on many conversations in my life where I could have said something differently or not said anything at all. *I should have acted with more empathy and grace. I could have been kinder.* I beat myself up and fill with shame as I realize I am not the peacemaker I wish to be. Some days I feel overwhelmed by toxic shame.

On a first visit to a therapist, she asked me to tell her my story, starting at the beginning. When I finished the summary of my story, she told me not to be so hard on myself. It was understandable it would be hard to turn those automatic reels off. After all—I was a child when I was in the cult. It made me feel better to receive her empathy and understanding. She didn't try to fix it or solve it. She just cared. She didn't think I was crazy or manic or bipolar or any of those conditions. I was just sad. *It's OK to be sad. It's just an emotion. I don't have to always hide it.*

I understand what my mother used to say, that we shouldn't air our dirty laundry, but sometimes we need to cry out for help. We need to let ourselves be open and vulnerable, whether it is to seek help for ourselves or because by telling our truths someone else will be touched and encouraged. Life is sometimes a comedy and sometimes it is a drama. It's OK to feel guilty and do a bit of self-examination and growth. That's a good thing. But when I feel shame, it's not about an act of wrongdoing—it's that my very existence is wrong. It's dark and hopeless. It's toxic.

At one time my husband and I were both in very dark places at the same time. It was so bad that for a split second, we considered a suicide pact. We were drowning in dark stormy water. I screamed at Oscar, "Don't you see me out here sinking? Can't you at least throw me a life preserver?"

I thought that maybe I saw him toss me one, but when I looked it didn't have a rope on it and he just walked away. *How will we survive? It is so dark in our lives. Where has the light gone? I can't hear any music.*

Then one day, standing in our garage, we voiced our hopelessness out loud and somehow hearing the words we were jolted and we realized the gravity of the situation. We were broken and scared standing there in the middle of our dream. In that moment, we looked in each other's eyes and saw love. Maybe the Beatles said it best when they said, 'all you need is love.' We needed to help each other and I thank God that the miracle of love helped us step back into the light.

Instinct led us to reach out and surround ourselves by the strong faithful friends in our lives. I knew we needed help. I reached out to my pastor for some personal counseling and Oscar reached out to help offered at the Veteran's Administration. It took time to get back into the game of life. I began by starting each day looking in the mirror and telling myself: *You can do this. You are OK. You are invincible. You are capable. You are precious.* I just needed to turn the top soil, dig down under the surface and uncover the roots of resilience and overcoming that were there. I heard God's whisper, telling me that He loved me just the way I was. I felt the warm embrace of my brothers when we went to California for a wedding. We had the chance to spend time with some of Oscar's old shipmates and see in their eyes the respect and tenderness they had for him. While God was whispering in my heart, I was seeing Him in my loved ones. The power of that combined love helped me keep my head above the water.

Years later, a therapist told me that I likely suffered from a mild form of post-traumatic stress disorder caused by the traumas of the cult years and the terrible grief of losing my children. I didn't know much about PTSD in general and so I didn't see the correlation or recognize the triggers that would ignite my anxiety and fears. It helps to have a gentle hand to remind me that everything is going to be all right. I know it myself from my own history and ability to overcome and thrive, but my mind plays tricks on me. If I just hold on and focus on what is real and what is not, the episode will pass. That's a strategy taught for dealing with PTSD.

I am grateful for the resilience wrought in me through misfortune and trauma; I have sharpened my ability to adapt and overcome obstacles and find my emotional strength. I know I must summon my own inner strength, but I also find it helpful to spend time with my close friends and family. When I look in their eyes, I can see their love and acceptance reflecting light and hope, which helps remind me of who I am and the light that lives in me. It's one reason I find community so vital. Communing with each other, with a willingness to be open and vulnerable, allows us to see into each other's hearts and to lift each other up.

It took a few years to recover from the state of shock we experienced from the emotional trauma of despair. I still struggle with deep feelings of being unlovable. I find it an amazing miracle that not only God loves me, but my friends love me too. Their powerful love carries me along, moving me forward; their collective friendship is as powerful as a river, an ocean and the wind and as timeless as the sands of the earth.

My childhood had been lonesome and solitary, but my adult life is rich and full of friends. I am surrounded by women and men comfortable in their own skins, safe and secure, able to appreciate beauty and give back to their families and communities. They are strong, compassionate, sensitive and kind people. They are willing to lend a hand or lend an ear, sharing and caring for each other and the generations that surround them. I learn so much by observing how gracefully they navigate the paths of their lives. The wind blows and they bend, but they do not break.

I cherish the threads of friendship with my dearest friends from my commune days, which have remained constant; neither time nor miles have unraveled the bonds we share. We share deep wounds and battle scars, but we've shared laughter too. We've shared the kind of friendship that is full of trust and rooted in faith, not only in God, but in each other. We share not only history, but also the current events of our lives. It has required a lot of effort for us to maintain those bonds, but there's a deep strong love that keeps us going. I am grateful and blessed.

We call one of our friends a saint. She laughs when she hears us refer to her that way. But she and her husband are such dear wonderful people. They took care of their parents with tenderness and laughter. They do so much volunteer work and yet always make time for friends too. With other friends, we share a love of travel, cooking and games. We watch out for each other. We cry with each other and we laugh. Boy, do we laugh. My mother used to say that if you have more friends than you can count on one hand, you are rich. Well, then, I am very wealthy as I have many friends, some new and some old. They are smart and strong, active and full of life. They are engaging. They are role models and heroes in my life. They complete me and encourage me by word and example.

The journey through darkness had been exhausting and confusing, but I focused on balancing the scales of my life by attending to the daily strategies I already knew, like gardening, entertaining, traveling and spending time with my dear friends and family. When the day was over and it was time to brush our teeth and get ready for bed, Oscar and I would stand together in front of the mirror and revisit the day or share a quiet thought. I remember distinctly the evening I looked in the mirror at Oscar and said, "See, if you hadn't fought the cancer, you wouldn't have been able to meet your great-grandson." At other times a touch of our hands reminds us of the miracle of choosing life.

As I write this, I feel mature and equipped to overcome the battles when the thoughts get dark. I don't see suicide as a solution for emotional pain anymore. It was startling to discover that it was burrowed in the recesses of my mind as an option. It's braver to work my way through it...to find my way to the light, to speak my pain out loud and get some help. We seek a doctor for a virus or a tooth ache, why not for sadness and distress? It's OK to get help.

Our nation has suffered a lot during the shutdown of COVID, fueling depression that now runs more rampant than ever before. So much of our internal struggle, pain and depression stems from isolation. We need to feel heard. It's important to share our pain.

Please hear my voice. Please call out if you need help. Please listen to those around you to see if they need help. I thank God that I am alive and not alone. Every moment of my life has been an invitation to learn. *I have not come this far to give up. This is another chance to choose life and overcome the challenges I face.*

Faith and Miracles

When I think about the challenges of my ancestors, including my parents and those before them that I did not know, I recognize how their ingenuity and strength has been passed down through my blood. I may not go to temple or follow the Jewish faith, but make no mistake about it, I am proud of my heritage and I take comfort in seeing the resemblance, physically and spiritually, and knowing that their resilience lives on in me.

My children never knew their grandfather, but my son looks so much like my dad. Over the years I've told him that when I look in his face, I see my dad. This one time...I needed a hug and so my strong, sweet, wise, faithful son took me in his arms and embraced me close to his heart. As I held on, I felt him pass some of his faith to me. I leaned back and looked up into his face and with tears in my voice I said, "I see more than just my dad when I look in your face, I see the face of God."

We gazed into each other's eyes for a moment and then he said, "Mom, you're just looking into a mirror."

That moment meant everything to me; it was so full of grace and love. It was a miracle, an absolute miracle. We could see God in each other and we were present in the moment willing to be vulnerable and open.

Everywhere I go, I look for God in the faces of those around me. I weave my faith together with community because each face holds a personal story, history and a glimpse of God.

This one time...Oscar and I were on a retreat of sorts, by a lake. We sat on the secluded dock, peacefully discussing our hearts' desires and our vision for our future. All of a sudden, I noticed a bush on the water's edge.

"Do you see that?" I asked Oscar.

"What?" he replied.

"You see it don't you? That bush looks like it's burning!"

We gazed upon it for a long time. The breeze on the lake was tumbling the light in and around the bush. It really did appear to be on fire, making me think of Moses and his burning bush.

"I wonder what God is saying through that bush?"

Without hesitation Oscar said, "I couldn't hear, you're talking too much!"

We cracked up laughing. What wisdom there was in that observation! I ask God to give me a sign or to tell me His desire and He tries, but am I listening?

I am working on the art of listening.

I try to hear God's desire for me. I know that if I follow His lead, it will be right. But hearing His voice can be difficult.

This one time...I asked my son, "how does one know, really *know*, if it's God's voice?"

"When the phone rings and you recognize the person's voice on the other end, it's the same," he replied wisely. "Spend time in prayer and reading and you will recognize His voice."

Oscar and I were finding our way out of the darkness, but I knew that we needed to continue to climb to higher ground. I knew that the women in my circle of friends could help me. We all shared tips about our homes, our bodies and matters of the heart. I knew these friends were people of faith. I'm not talking about their religion or what church they attended—I could tell that they loved God by how they loved their families, friends and neighbors.

During my single years, I attended a few church services, but usually I couldn't stay until the end without something triggering alarms inside of me and I would bolt. Then I met Oscar and he practiced his strong faith with daily spiritual readings and prayers. It helped me and I felt a crack in my heart open to listen for God.

Oscar practiced his faith in a Catholic setting. I knew nothing of that religion but I agreed to attend services with him. I liked the ritualistic format, with robes and incense. I liked the act of prayers recited out loud in unison and I loved kneeling in prayer. Oscar and I attended Catholic mass every Sunday for twenty years, starting each week with a church service on Sunday. Looking back, it was a necessary phase in my spiritual journey. It provided the space for me to get comfortable with being inside a church. It was good to have a designated time to pray, and it was good family time.

However, there was something lacking. I was not permitted to participate, because not only was I not Catholic, I was divorced. I could have hidden it, but I still would have known. Catholicism doesn't allow divorcées to receive the weekly communion. Communion is the distribution of bread and wine to the congregation as a remembrance of the last Passover supper that Jesus observed and shared with his disciples, when he passed the bread and wine and said "Take and eat, this is my body and blood given for you." Remembering that the body and blood of Jesus was offered up as a Passover sacrifice helps us to reflect on his death and the extent of his love. Each time I receive communion I feel right there at the cross with Jesus and it is a very meaningful and personal experience.

At that point though, all that stood out was that we were not allowed to participate. When the entire congregation rose, pew by pew, to approach the altar in single file and receive communion, Oscar and I stayed seated. We stood out like sore thumbs. For those few moments every week, the shame of my past would revisit me. It was as if I travelled back in time, sitting on a tree stump at the commune announcing my shame to all.

One evening we accepted an invitation for an intimate dinner at the home of our dear friends Darlene and Al Weddle. Over cocktails and appetizers, the men sat in the living room talking about their latest projects while Darlene and I visited around the kitchen island getting the last-minute dinner preparations ready. All day I looked forward to the visit with Darlene—a friend with whom I could feel totally myself and accepted. Darlene is a caring friend and a great conversationalist. A skilled listener, she has the art of making everyone comfortable. I knew I could tell her anything, but I didn't know where to start. She knew about Oscar's cancer journey and my latest concerns about post-polio syndrome, but I hadn't told her just how dark our lives were behind closed doors.

"It's been three months since we went to church," I began. "I feel so bad that no one from our church has called to check on us."

"Oh Adrienne," she said, "you need to come to church with us!"

I knew Darlene was right. It was time for us to find another church.

"Oscar will feel right at home," she added, "because our evangelical Lutheran church follows the same format as a Catholic service, but they accept divorce and invite everyone to share in communion."

I felt hugged just by the thought of it.

"Yes, I'd like that very much," I told her.

The next Sunday we met Darlene and Al at their church, held in a small, simple chapel. The chapel was quaint and the people were warm and welcoming. That day, I knew I had found my way home. I needed a place where I could relax, be myself, and explore my faith and my connection to God.

Many years ago, when my son was about eight years old, he asked, "why don't you go to church?"

"Do you know how sometimes people get mad at each other?" I replied. "Well, I'm mad at God."

It took a long time, but one day I realized I wasn't mad at God anymore. I knew He didn't make the bad things happen in my life. He was there to be my friend, father and confidant, guiding me with love, peace and wisdom. Certainly, my life had been filled with some difficult circumstances, but I also see clearly the many blessings I've enjoyed. My cup was full with loving Oscar, loving children and grandchildren and the dearest of friends and my gosh, how lucky I was to have had a life filled with wonderful adventures. My heart was also filled with thanksgiving and gratitude to my God, who never gave up and stayed by my side through my wild times, doubts and anger.

At last, I was open to life again. The light was shining brightly and I felt safe to contemplate my beliefs about God and faith and miracles. Being a part of this new church family provided much needed nourishment to the seed of my faith that had been planted in my soul so many years earlier. Open conversations challenged me and helped me to grow and mature in my faith. We were back on a path in an open loving place of acceptance and grace, after surviving a very dark period.

I still struggle from the trauma and sadness that lives inside of me. When I don't feel all sunshine and smiles, I feel a bit guilty; why can't I just let go and trust and be joyous and grateful in all things? After all, I have God on my side. He's proven it to me time and time again. I don't know if it's doubt or depression or grief, but I think I shouldn't put so much pressure on myself to always feel up and positive. God loves me just the way I am, when I'm happy and when I'm sad. I know I need to trust God.

Let me be clear—it is not shameful to admit weakness and ask for help. Absolutely talk to God, but you can also call a friend or a doctor or a hotline. Don't be afraid to speak up and ask for help. I know now that I do not need to be guilty or ashamed for experiencing a valid emotion like sadness. As an apostle of Jesus shared, "If our hearts condemn us, we know that God is greater than our hearts and he knows everything" (1 John 3:20). If God doesn't condemn me, I will try not to condemn myself. A seedling takes time to develop roots and become a mature tree with fruit or shade for a weary soul. So too my faith is living, growing and evolving. *I choose to remember just how much God values me and to try to value myself equally, with compassion. I hear the music. I'm listening. I choose to dance. I choose life.*

My faith is the belief that we are created for a personal relationship with God. I hear his gentle calling regularly and accept the graceful invitation again and again to get reacquainted with my God. He stands silently by my side at all times calling me into the light. Paul, an early disciple of Jesus, writes that "faith is the substance of things hoped for, the evidence of things not seen." When I feel hope stirring inside me, I recognize it is the evidence of my ability to transcend the struggles and overcome. My joy is in the acknowledgement that while I am broken, God loves me just the way I am. The circumstances of my life left deep scars, but they also gave me opportunities to confront the empty corners in myself and surrender to the refining process of perseverance and character. Faith is not about rules or religion. It's about love and hope.

How I feel and what I know about God has evolved through the years. Many religions have what they believe to be absolutes and those are fine, but in relationships and life the answers aren't always black and white. The world has a lot of grey, as do matters of the heart and faith. I see a lot of grey and I don't believe it's so important that I know the absolute truths or define the hair-splitting details in black and white. I'm never going to agree with every doctrine of a specific religion, nor will I ever understand it all, but that doesn't mean I can't have faith and participate. Participating is part of community and if I choose not to join in because I don't agree with every detail, then to me it's kind of like throwing out the baby with the bath water. Religion and faith are two different things and I'm talking about faith now. My personal faith is like a quilt made up of cut up little pieces put back together, creating a unique and beautiful piece of art.

In my journey I've learned essential strategies that have helped me triumph and cope with adversity. I must pursue my creative passions, cultivate my faith and spend time with my community. These things are tightly woven together, infusing energy into my life and bringing me peace. I believe that my desire to carve out time and space to explore the passions that call to me are whispers from God encouraging me and cheering me on, saying, "Fear not, go ahead, just try, you can do it."

In our world today, dealing with COVID and anger from a polarized political climate, I believe there is a lot depression and hostility. We need to help each other to rise above to a place of light and kindness and purpose. We only get one time to live this life. My creative passions, faith and community are the waters that keep my soul hydrated. If I distance myself from any of these things for too long, I become parched and dry. I want to be challenged and enriched and live with open eyes and an open heart. It's my way of navigating through my rich and busy life. As an introvert by nature, I need to refuel after spending time with folks. I need to manage my energy levels. The forces of my passions and my community push me to drink of the water of life. If I fill up my cup, then it can overflow to others in my community, be it family, friends, church, or neighbors.

I believe that most often miracles take place in our hearts and minds. We witness miracles all day long without ever realizing it. Every time you see two people holding hands, whether a parent and child or a husband and wife, siblings or even best friends, there is a story that is held and woven between those hands and surely that's a miracle. In the good times and bad, I'm able to pray and connect to God and that is a miracle. Many people pray for a miracle of healing from a disease or imminent death, and I suppose that is fine, because God can do anything. Sometimes I pray for physical healings, but I believe the miracle is in finding peace and acceptance—what will be will be. Finding peace in death is a miracle. Finding the way out of the darkness is a miracle. Giving and receiving forgiveness is a miracle. Giggling children, the change of seasons, modern medicine, hopeful hearts, or just the ability to take a walk, these are the miracles that surround us every day. *I want to keep my eyes and heart open to see miracles every day.*

When I saw the face of God in my son's face and he replied that I was just looking in a mirror, it was also a confirmation of why I feel community is so vital. When we try to see God in each other with grace and love, isn't that what God is all about? We are here to love one another regardless of our ethnicity, politics, socio-economic class or religion. Who am I? I am a child of God. I am called to participate in a relationship with God, to live by faith and love my neighbor. That might look differently for different people. It is not my job to cast judgment. I'll leave it to God to figure out the details.

Nurturing my personal relationship with God is important to me. I see Him in the flowers in my garden and the dirt that protects the tender roots. When I have my hands in that dirt, stretching my body to its limits and relaxing my mind for meditation, I feel closer to God. Digging in the dirt is one of my favorite creative outlets. That hint or challenge to learn to garden has enriched the rest of my life. South Texas soil can be hard as a rock and plants don't do well in hard dirt. Using tools and my bare hands I turn the soil, making soft dirt to give the tender roots freedom to spread and grow. As I dig, I listen for God and I hear Him say, "Harden not your heart." I feel connected to Him as I plant seeds and tend the plants, pruning them and guiding their growth. It reminds me that I am made in His image, able to artistically plant and grow and create beauty as He did. His wondrous creations call me into an intimate place of worship.

When Oscar and I were outside working in the yard, neighbors would stop by and visit. Who would think that the quiet hard work of turning the soil and planting in the earth would also cultivate our neighborhood friendships? We would stop to share a story or hear news and take the time to share a clipping from an admired plant or flower. It was a marvelous way to combine time to listen for God, a passion for the dirt and nurturing connection to community.

It's also important to take time to be still and reflect, connecting to the prayers that live in my soul. Sometimes those prayers don't even have words, they're just longings or groans buried deep in my heart. Perhaps they are the molecules and atoms that I sometimes feel stirring and moving inside of me. *I yearn for a closer relationship with you, God.* When I allow my heart to rest on the memory of a person or place that has touched me—that is a prayer. Sometimes my conversation with God consists of words spoken out loud, but sometimes it is just the stillness of my being that is the prayer. "Be still and know that I am God" (Psalms 46:10).

It is medically proven that community and social connections help us mentally and spiritually. It helps me draw nearer to God watching Him work through community. There are no words that can describe the inspiration and faith I receive from seeing God in my family and friends. I watch with awe as my older friends navigate with grace and strength all the challenges that life as an older adult brings. Despite having seen war and death of loved ones and illness and pain, they carry on and continue living life to the fullest. They dig deep and find pleasure and happiness, contentment and purpose. Just knowing them gives me strength. I am grateful because they have allowed me in to share their stories and know the journeys they have taken.

I am also inspired by the energy of the young people to be curious and inquisitive, finding their passions and working through their fears and weaknesses to find the things that bring them joy. They are just starting out on their spiritual path of finding their purpose. When we gather and share, I see grace and love in action and that fills me with faith and hope. Healing happens in community.

Now, after all these years, I trust my intuition and choices and reflect with empathy on my own life. I didn't necessarily follow a prescribed typical script, but my choices and creative passions, along with my faith and community, carry me down the river to a place of endless possibilities. I made my own story and I feel brave for having done so. Life is bittersweet, but I am living a wonderful abundant life and transcending the odds. *Thank you for my ability to use my faith every day, not to control but to be free. I feel courage inside of me. I wake up every day renewed, excited and ready for whatever comes my way.*

After years of cult indoctrination and years of being angry with God, now I just want to live in peace with God and those around me. I have come back to a simple foundation of believing we are saved by grace through faith, not through works or anything we do. Grace is for everyone—a free gift for the whole world. I know that my personal response to that gift of grace encourages me to find ways to live a better life and give back to my community and the world. We don't need to judge others; each person is complicated and only God truly knows their heart. Perhaps a person gives back in the simple way they share a smile or a kind word.

I recall a discussion with a friend with disabilities, who was asking, "What if I can't help with a hammer or serve a meal to someone in need?" He felt bad being confined and restricted by his disabilities.

I offered him comfort saying, "God knows our hearts and we can offer our grateful response of thanksgiving in many different ways. Perhaps say a prayer for someone or offer a kind word."

Many religions are work-oriented but I believe we are reconciled to God by grace. We just need to have open hearts to experience God's marvelous grace. My faith is more about relationship than doctrine. I try to have an open heart to what else God might have in store for me. I am able to forgive myself and see my scars as honor and beauty.

It was at that small church in Conroe, Texas that I fell in love with God all over again. The members welcomed me. They were curious and inquisitive about my outlook as a Jewish girl who had spent time in a religious cult and then so many years in a Catholic church. We shared open conversations and I felt loved with each encounter. Hope was alive in my heart. I loved the music, which was lively and included songs that were familiar. Music brings my emotions to the surface, giving me the ability to express with tears of sadness or dancing joy. I love to feel the music and the rhythm, even though I can't carry a tune or sing a note. In fact, I once had a priest say to me, "You know, Mrs. Poppe, it's OK to lip sync." That's how bad my singing is, but I feel the vibrations and get the rhythm flowing in my body and the music becomes therapy. With the contemporary sound of guitars and tambourines, I found myself swaying to the music and feeling glad to be alive.

Then one night I had a dream about sewing and quilts. The next morning at church coffee hour I sat with a dear new friend, Barbara, and her face lit up when I told her about my dream that we should make quilts for the world. For many years she dreamed that our church would have a quilting ministry. Little did I know that there was an established, nationwide, Lutheran World Relief ministry that made and donated over 500,000 quilts a year as part of disaster relief. That morning Barbara and I committed to each other to help our congregation join the World Relief efforts. It was magnificent. We asked for donations of fabric and set a time to gather. We received old shirts and gently worn sheets, and someone donated old books of upholstery samples. Tediously removing the cardboard, we ended up with squares of beautiful upholstery fabric, which we sewed together for mosaic quilts that represented our love. These quilts would act perhaps as a floor or a bed or a room divider, or giving warmth to someone who had just survived a disaster. As we stitched, we hoped and prayed that the love woven in the threads would be delivered to someone in need of it. I'm really not sure who was more blessed, the recipients or us—we found such joy and purpose in the scraps and threads of our quilts.

One time, I confided in the young pastor of that small congregation that I lived with quite a lot of shame. Pastor Lorin asked me a life-changing question: "Where do you find the most peace?"

I hesitated and then answered, "In front of my sewing machine."

He told me to spend more time there. I took him up on that wise advice and found my way to the greatest passion I have ever known: quilting.

Quilting is a historical art, the practice of using every scrap of fabric to make beautiful and functional quilts. Over the years, quilting has changed, morphing by the 1980's into a multi-million dollar worldwide industry. There is so much to learn and so many wonderful generous women and men willing to share their talents. It has been exciting for me to learn the skills and see the various styles.

Houston Texas hosts the largest annual International Quilt Festival in the world. It has thousands of quilts on exhibit, as well as hundreds of vendors and classes. Since I only lived an hour from Houston, it was an event I attended many times even before I was a quilter, just to admire the fabulous quilts. What I saw astounded me. The world of quilts no longer consists of just the traditional pieced quilts of our grandmothers. Oh, there were plenty of those, done with the highest caliber of precision, but there were also displays of highly unusual artistic quilts. There are many categories, including traditional quilts, modern quilts, hand-stitched quilts, machine-sewn quilts, themed quilts, embellished quilts, landscape quilts, portrait quilts and custom-designed quilts.

This one time...just after the start of the world relief quilting ministry at our church, I went with several church ladies to the Houston International Quilt Festival. As I walked around, I was again in awe of the magnificent artistry, details and thought that went into these exquisite pieces. I was gasping and grabbing my heart. *Oh my. Oh my. Oh my.* I could feel the passion growing inside of me. It takes days to see the entire festival, but we only had one day. In the morning, we viewed the exhibits. Sometimes we were lucky enough to come upon a quilt when the artist was standing beside it. What a delight to hear firsthand the stories of what inspired these artists to design the quilts, and how many hours were spent in the making. After about five hours, we took a break before hitting the aisles and aisles of vendors, looking for hidden treasure.

Then I saw her—a finished piece on display, a pattern by Nancy Mullen, called *If Mary Had Been a Quilter*. The piece was 30" x 44" with a silhouette of Mary sitting with baby Jesus in her arms wrapped in a quilt. I knew instantly that she was the treasure for which I had been searching. I bought the pattern as a gift for my sister in Idaho, who was already quilting. My friends encouraged me to keep her for myself, and when I told my sister about the pattern, she ordered it for herself. A few months later I flew to Boise for a quilting retreat where my sister and I each made our versions of *If Mary Had Been a Quilter*.

When I first saw the pattern, I thought it was about Jesus, but when the piece was done, I thought maybe it was more about Mary. What was Mary thinking? How did Mary feel? I felt empathy in my heart for her. How was it that she could carry and raise Jesus? She was a willing servant of God.

Mary introduced me to the world of art quilts and inspired me in so many ways. I was thirsty for knowledge to improve my abilities in this newfound creative passion. Creating the quilts, learning about threads and fabrics and patterns and techniques infused me with joy and energy. I couldn't believe that I had found another passion. I already loved to garden and cook, entertain and travel, finding those things to be artful in nature and spiritual, if done in the right frame of mind. With quilting I knew I was stepping up my game. If you want me to light up, ask me about my quilts. I knew I was not just dabbling in something; quite the contrary, this was a calling to begin a new creative journey. Quilting filled up mind, body and soul, giving me a way to give back to my loved ones and community not only with the actual quilts, but by finding my light and therefore being able to engage and share with more joy.

I believe that creative outlets are the antidote for the ills of the soul and society. Creativity helps my mind and heart to be engaged, like a child learning and eager to explore. It gives me energy that is powerful and electric, filling me with hope and joy and giving me the tools to cope with my trauma and difficulties. These passions seem to be gentle invitations from God to a place of peace and contentment. They fill my days and nights. I love to dig in the dirt and see things grow. I love to cook and bake and have delicious smells fill the house with anticipation. I love every detail of entertaining, creating an environment ripe for intimate storytelling and sharing. I love the mental challenge and friendly bonds during a card game. I love the absorbing details of travel, from the dreaming and planning to the actual journey. I love being anchored each week with my church family. I am passionate about quilting. My life is abundantly full and I am filled with gratitude.

My evolution has been slow at times, but slow and steady wins the race. I often say life is not a sprint, it's a marathon, so I need to pace myself so I can be in it for the long haul. My faith transcends time and space. Perhaps I did have times of doubt when my faith wasn't strong, but maybe, just maybe, God remembers only the times my faith was bold and strong, because he forgives the rest. My faith helped me find my way through each and every struggle.

If you met me at a juncture in my life when perhaps it was the winter of my soul, rather than the spring, I regret I didn't show you the fruits of my faith, giving love or kindness or generosity. I am sorry that my struggle with self-doubt and shame spilled over to some folks and pushed them away. My heart is so full of love for each and every one and I pray for the miracle of forgiveness and healing in broken relationships that still exist. I still stumble, but it doesn't take me quite as long to get up, brush myself off and get back in the game.

I don't fight the current so much anymore, because my coping skills help me to relax into the flow, moving gracefully through the river of my life. *May I be a willing servant.*

Oscar's six children, about 2017

Nathan, me and Leah, Mother's Day 2019.

Fear Not

A storm was brewing off the coast of Africa. On September 1, 2008 it was declared a tropical depression, about 1,700 miles east of Puerto Rico. Gaining strength as it moved, a few days later it became a named storm, Ike. By September 7th it was a Category 4 hurricane heading for the US, causing havoc at each island it slammed into. Crossing islands slowed Ike down, but as the storm continued west, it stalled in the Gulf of Mexico and began to intensify again.

When we were Florida residents, we stayed and survived the 1992 Category 5 Hurricane Andrew, which devastated Homestead, Florida. Subsequently, we were evacuated from many hurricanes. Oscar and I respect the power of a hurricane. As a man of the sea, Oscar is always tuned in to storm activities. He has been in hurricanes at sea on small ships. When we moved from Florida to Texas, we hoped our inland location would help us escape the impact of the hurricanes that had threatened us for years as coastal residents. However, a large hurricane can have a bandwidth of 100 miles or more as it moves inland, enough to affect our Texas home 100 miles from the coast.

Water plays an important role in the life of our body and our planet; the cycle of water never ceases to amaze me. Drinking water allows our heart to relax and not work so hard, pumping oxygen and filling our cells and body with energy. The power of water is immense. A slow drip over time can destroy a building or move the earth. When it comes to a hurricane, warm water is the energy source for the storm, giving it strength and power. The water that is essential in our life for our health and wellbeing is a double-edged sword as it also fuels the destructive force of a hurricane. As Ike headed to Galveston, we stayed alert, reminding each other of God's most often repeated command: "Fear not."

As we waited, we remembered the time when Hurricane Rita came to visit, a few years earlier. Oscar's Aunt Joann asked if we could help her sister Bonnie in Beaumont, Texas, along with her husband and her very elderly mother, who was under hospice care and required oxygen. They needed a place to evacuate that would maintain electricity for the oxygen tanks their mom needed. Our RV had a generator.

"Can you take them in?" asked Aunt Joann.

"Of course we can," we said.

There's quite a lot to think about and do to prepare for a hurricane. We didn't have to make bags of sand to lay around the edge of our home, nor did we need to board up our windows, as those who live by the water's edge do. We began by securing everything outside, because it might become a flying projectile in a storm. We gathered supplies, including water for drinking and flushing toilets along with batteries and cash, because ATMs don't work without electricity. We filled the cars with gasoline, gathered radios, flashlights, tools, and canned goods.

The next day we were ready for our houseguests. Bumper to bumper traffic from the one-way evacuation north left them exhausted but relieved to be at our home. We settled everyone in, showing them their rooms, and sat down to have a bite to eat and gather our calm. Jimmie had served in World War II in the Philippines and was at the battle of Corregidor. Somehow he ended up spending two years in the jungles avoiding capture. He was a good person to have with you during a hurricane, as he was full of stories and calm strength.

Bonnie and I sat on the screen porch for a bit listening to the wind and rain. We held hands and prayed, grateful for being together. The storm was predicted to hit in the wee hours of the morning, so we decided to get some rest, knowing that we might need our energy later. We hugged goodnight. About 1 a.m. the howling wind woke us up, and we realized we had lost electricity. We needed to move everyone to the RV where the generator could power the vital oxygen tank. I scurried to the RV to make up the beds. The dinette became a full size bed for Jimmie and Bonnie and the couch flipped out to a twin bed for mom. Under the cloud of darkness in the wind and rain, we moved across the driveway to the RV. OMG. We realized we couldn't lift the oxygen tank up the RV stairs. Reluctantly, we went across the street and knocked on our young neighbor's door and asked for help. He came out and lifted the tank into the RV. Thank goodness for neighbors and generators. *Lord, please let us get some sleep.*

About an hour later, we were awakened to the shrill beeping of an alarm. I nudged Oscar awake. The engine rooms aboard all those ships of his youth had stolen his hearing years ago.

"Honey, what is that?"

"It's the CO_2 alarm in the RV."

"What the heck?"

We told our guests they had to move back into the house. "It isn't safe to stay out here."

There was one portable oxygen tank that would get mom through until noon the next day. We'd figure something out. The next morning the storm passed and we were spared. We made some calls to local medical supply stores and found grace when an owner answered her store phone. She wasn't in town because she evacuated to Dallas, but she would have an employee meet us there and give us a few extra portable tanks to hold us over. She didn't ask for money or paperwork, she just offered a helping hand. This is what love in action looks like.

As we waited for Hurricane Ike we found calm in remembering that we survived Rita with neighbors helping neighbors. Prepared, Oscar and I held hands and listened for the still small voice of God, saying again, "Fear not."

The outer bands of Ike passed over our home, but remarkably we incurred only a small amount of damage. We started the process of clean up. There are so many reasons that no man should be or could be an island. We need community whether we admit it or not. We are linked by our human condition with our unique and differing qualities and called to support each other as one family. Our family and community of friends scattered across the world were concerned about us, so I sent a letter to let them know how we had fared through yet another hurricane.

Hello dear friends and family,

Thank you for all your prayers and loving thoughts. We are ok. We are more than ok. Here's our little world experience.

As we told you, we were prepared....and so we calmly waited. The eye of Ike passed maybe 25 miles to the east of our home.

We are safe. Our house has no structural damage. Just tore up our screen porch, which Oscar and a neighbor have already repaired. Also lost some landscaping, which Adrienne has already dug up. We had some minor damage to our RV, when a tree fell on it. Unfortunately, after it fell on the RV, then it hit Oscar's truck. It is drivable—just has the back window out and the left rear fender and rear cab top that will need to be replaced.

It's weird to see our house fine and around us trees in roofs and huge trees pulled out by the roots, lying on their side. We almost feel guilty for having everything so back to normal.

Things like this bring out the best and worst in mankind and show who are good neighbors. We are very, very blessed. Our property did look like a bomb went off, with trees in neighbors' houses and down trees blocking access to the street and no electricity, no water, no phones (land or cell). EVERYONE pitched in immediately. We had strong young neighbors helping move trees and drag debris to the edge of our property so it could be picked up. Neighbors were bringing us coffee, sharing food, hugs, stories and even ice. We helped feed everyone one night, then they'd feed us the next. We lent batteries. They lent a charger for a battery.

We had water within a few days. Last night we got electricity and phone. Today we got cable! Today Adrienne was back to work and life is getting back to normal.

Some odd things you don't think about...like the nest of bees that are disturbed by the weather and so while you battle all the other things then there are bees. The windows are open so the lovebugs are even in the refrigerator that had to be open to air. Our ankles are spotted from the red ant bites from stepping in piles while cleaning up. My feet are full of blisters from the water shoes worn while cleaning up. We are so blessed. We have water shoes and a house to clean up.

You don't think about the little things like you can't get cell phone service, so you want to drive to find a connection to a tower, but you don't want to use gas, because there is none. It was a delight to get gas today with no line. We filled up.

The sound of the washing machine is nice. It means clean clothes.

I am thankful to have a job to go back to. Some are not so lucky. The economic snowball of an event like this is endless. In our office, now we hope for local banks and offices to be able to open up so we get business to conduct in our office that is still standing.

We are rambling and tired, but good and blessed and love you each. Let's catch up soon.

Love, The Poppes

It took a month to get everything back in order. My precious flowerbeds took quite a beating but thankfully most of the plants and flowers survived. The support of our friends, family and community helped us to weather this hurricane, just like they provide vital support and help to us in every one of life's storms.

Taking a deep breath and exhaling, I was ready to allow myself to get excited for the November reunion we'd planned before the storm, inviting my three siblings and their spouses for a gathering at our house. Most often we reunited on the West Coast, so I was eager to share the warmth of our Texas home with my brothers and sister. Since I love to open my home with the spirit of hospitality, it meant so much to me to be able to share this with them. My essence is reflected in the details of my home: its comfortable seating, the pictures of my ancestors and memorabilia and art that adorn every wall. I wanted to share that with my family. My son and daughter were driving down from Dallas to join us. We had plenty of room to sleep everyone using the RV as guest quarters. It would be three nights of wonderful togetherness. We all like each other very much and recognize how special that is, because not all families are like that.

I get so much strength from my brothers and sister. Although we have lived far from each other most of my life, nevertheless we share a bond of indescribable respect and love for each other that fills my heart with courage and warmth. Letting my mind rest on every memory stored in my soul and keenly aware of the grace bestowed on Oscar and me as survivors of darkness, cancer and hurricanes, I searched for words to express my feelings to my family as I wrote the following letter, which I read out loud to them on our first night together.

Dear Ones,

It seems I've been counting wake-ups my whole life. Filled with anticipation looking toward a joyous event, we count months, weeks, days, even single-digit wake-ups—until finally there are no more wake-ups.

This morning the house is quiet and it smells delicious. The months and days and hours of planning, preparing and travelling are over—it's here.

All around the world, all year long families have events and gatherings, joyous and otherwise, for which they count wake-ups.

This time, this one time...here in our world on Hydra Court in Willis, Texas, our celebration is great. We are gathered for no other reason than to express our love.

We are grateful—so very grateful for a day in 1919 when Leonard Albert Sholdar was born, a day in 1921 when Luella Gobetz was born, and a day in 1940 when Leonard met Luella and married her two weeks later.

The rich inheritance they joined and passed down was a wealth of qualities of honesty, hard work, honor, loyalty, strength, character, courage, humility and love.

Well, Dad might not have always been honest—like when he told Mom he had a job and money in the bank so she would marry him—but then she found out otherwise. But he never made me doubt the honesty of his love.

They were hard workers, finding their way to provide food, clothes, and houses, and more houses, and bikes. They taught us by example and words to give "a good day's work for a good day's pay."

Our dad committed to his country to give them everything, even his life, if necessary. He fought in World War II for a better way of life for us. His silent honor lives on in us.

Henry Ford said, "Whether you think you can, or that you can't, you are usually right."

I don't remember many exact words or conversations or moments shared with my father and, recently my daughter asked me to share with her memories of a grandfather she never knew. I told her that my memories were only sad, but that was wrong. What I know and remember about my dad, and my mom, is the joy I feel when I think of them. I feel the strength of their spirits walking with me every day, letting me know I can do it.

I can walk with strength and courage and hard work. I can walk. I can do anything. I can live with love and character. I can be a character, because Luella showed us how. Her character lives on in us. I can live, and even die, with grace and dignity because they taught us adversity and distress are just moments, not lifetimes.

It is a rich inheritance to be part of the Gobetz/Sholdar family. I am so proud to be a part of them and of you. Welcome to our home, all the spouses too! All our Love.

After a moment of silence, there were tears and everyone stood to pass hugs all around as we all felt the love and the pride in our heritage that we share. It was a comfortable, warm and wonderful visit filled with storytelling and intimate conversations, not to mention the delicious meals we shared. I was so very grateful for the efforts of everyone to make the connections and the gathering happen.

After everyone left and we put things back in order, we rested up and were filled with energy to pour into our passion for travel. We did a rendezvous with family in Destin, Florida and we did a marvelous Colorado RV trip with our 13-year-old granddaughter, meeting up with friends and their RV. Life dealt us a second or third or fourth chance. A dear friend once told me, shaking her head, "you always land on your feet." Even I was amazed that we had jumped back into the game of life and landed upright. I was mindful of the importance of cultivating relationships to maintain my resilience.

The people and passions in my life were wonderful blessings and I was full of joy, but simultaneously underneath the surface, as often happens in life, there were losses also. One of Oscar's dearest friends, Ed Price, passed away. Oscar missed his friend so very, very much. We were honored to accompany his wife for a Coast Guard burial at sea. When I lose someone I love, my response is to reach out more for my other loved ones because I am keenly aware that I am not guaranteed tomorrow. Motivated to hug our loved ones, I continued planning and making visits, flying from coast to coast to see family and friends.

One of our grandsons joined the Army. We received a letter from him while he was in boot camp. He asked if Papa could still fit in his uniform? He would be honored to have him there at his boot camp graduation so that he could fulfill a life-long dream of being able to salute his grandfather. I wrote a letter in return promising to be there with Papa in uniform. As we prepared ourselves for travel, I found moments of stillness and clarity. *I am once again so very grateful that we chose life so that we could be here for moments like this. Tears of joy fill my heart for the tenderness and respect that exists between Papa and his grandson.* It was a marvelous event with the family seeing their father in his uniform, which he hadn't worn in over 20 years.

The next year we attended our granddaughter's wedding in Chicago. Some years earlier, when she was 24 years old, she had called to say she wanted time alone with us. She flew out and we took an RV trip to the ocean and had a whole week together, just she and us. It was a gift of love and connection for her to want to just be with us. We lifted each other up and promised to never let go. Now it was our delight to go and witness her joy and entry into her new life. When it was all over and we were getting ready for bed it was another occasion for me to look at Oscar and thank him for choosing life. I said to him, "See, since you fought the cancer and overcame, you were able to dance with your granddaughter at her wedding." The light of love shines through the darkness and wins again, filling our souls with warmth.

Another love story blossomed that year. My son called and said, "Mom, you won't believe it." The girl he had dated in high school, who had stolen his heart some 20 years earlier, looked him up on Facebook and they had a coffee date scheduled. "I'm not going to let her go again," he told me. Not long after they reconnected, he brought her down to Willis to meet us, because we hadn't met her in their high school days. Their love was so evident it was oozing from their pores.

Shortly after they left, I had an idea. I called Nathan and said I knew he might have something special or big in mind for a ring for the proposal, but there was something on my heart. I had a cocktail ring of my mother's with many diamonds in it, which all came from my grandmother and great-grandmother. None of the diamonds were of excellent quality, but it would bring me great joy if he wanted her to have a piece of our ancestry for his bride to be. He didn't hesitate, saying he would love that and so would she. A plan was hatched for him to pick out a setting and we would remove the diamond of his choice to be used in the ring.

A few months later Oscar and I accompanied him to the jewelry store. This was a big moment indeed. There were so many choices. Understandably, he was having a hard time making up his mind. Standing at the display case I said, "Let's go across the street and get a Scotch while you consider your choices."

The salesman, overhearing me, said, "Ma'am, no need to go across the street, we have a bottle of Scotch behind the counter for just these occasions."

We sat and had our Scotch while Nathan considered the moment. Finally, he was ready. He knew what he wanted to do. He looked over at me and said, "Mom, you won't believe this, but when I packed, I was so rushed and nervous I forgot my credit card." This was too funny. I told him that wasn't a problem, because

I knew he was good for it. With hearts full of love and hope for the future, our family diamond would be in the setting he picked for the beginning of a new life with endless possibilities.

Our hearts were listening during all these events to see how God was directing our path. We took a few other RV trips with friends and then we took one by ourselves to repeat a favorite loop trip revisiting New Mexico, Colorado and the Grand Canyon. It was a marvelous retreat as we viewed the majestic mountains and canyons. It never gets old. We enjoyed many hours of comfortable silence contemplating and listening.

When we got home from that trip, we made a huge life decision. It was time to sell the RV. We enjoyed many years of safe joyous traveling. Now, as we were getting older, it was harder to navigate the physical part of loading the RV, driving, parking and setting up camp. It was a difficult decision that I might equate to major surgery, but we knew it was the right thing to do. We didn't plan on giving up our passion for travel, and we were grateful for all the years we explored the nooks and crannies of our great country. Seeing the USA through the lens of RV travel allowed us to get up close and personal with this great nation that we live in. We started camping and RVing in the days of maps and pay phones and ended up in the age of GPS, cell phones and computers. We travelled a long way in miles and time. It was hard to say goodbye to our unit, which served us well and was pristine clean, as Oscar always tended the equipment well. We put a For Sale sign in the window and the very next day a newly retired couple came to look and bought her. We were so happy she would take another family on endless adventures.

Looking back, I realize it was just another opportunity to reinvent myself. It was time to reflect and choose how to spend my precious days. The coordinating, planning, budgeting and scheduling for our continuous RV trips took a lot of time and energy. Now my mind and heart had more room for other endeavors. I was spending more time with the World Relief quilting ministry and was very drawn to the world of colors, patterns and fabrics. It was a world that combined creative passion with a warm and generous community of women. I wanted to step through that open door and explore.

Then there was a doctor's visit where they asked me the standard question, "Have you fallen in the last year?" When I hesitated, Oscar spoke up and said, "Yes, she has."

In fact, I was falling more often. I thought of it as tripping really. Between my general practitioner and my post-polio doctor at the Texas Institute for Rehabilitation, we realized that my right foot had dropped. I was unaware that I had started to walk on the side of my foot, causing stress to my ankle.

Standing straight up on flat feet the doctor asked me to lift my toes toward the ceiling. No problem on my left foot. I could wiggle my toes to almost a 90 degree angle.

"Ok, now do that on your right foot," the doctor said.

"I'm trying." But I was unable to lift my right big toe off the floor, and that was a problem.

Lifting your big toe is the first unconscious part of taking a step. You cannot walk safely without being able to lift your big toe. Several doctors and physical therapists at the highest caliber hospitals told me there was nothing they could do. It was probably the result of the overuse I put my legs through with all the glorious years of dancing and hiking and exercise.

The solution was to put me back into a brace. They gave me a prescription for an AFO brace for drop foot to include a strap to help align my ankle. It was a horrible ugly thing. I cried and cried. I knew I was lucky to be in a city with amazing doctors and wonderful healthcare, but I cried over the loss of my beautiful wardrobe. I know it sounds silly and small, but I love fashion, from every day to dressing up for a formal affair. How could I do that with the bulky shoes I'd have to wear to fit over this brace? *I'll never be able to wear my cowboy boots again, or high heels. How will my life change? Breathe Adrienne. Fear Not. Give thanks for the strong years.*

I figured I'd learn to adapt. It wasn't long before I realized that the strap that went around my ankle to hold the plastic brace in place and support my foot was really hurting my ankle. We needed to discuss alternatives. A new DBS brace was recommended by the orthopedic specialist, made primarily out of titanium. It would be custom made for me and molded so that I would slip my lower leg into it; amazingly, it required no strapping, so there would be no pressure on my ankle. It went from under my toes, around my ankle, up the back of my calf and circled around my leg just under my knee. Though bulky, it was kind of cool and bionic-looking.

It was considered the Lamborghini of braces and it was questionable whether insurance would pay for it. We considered, we prayed, we took the counsel of our adult children and proceeded with the making of my custom brace. *I can do this. I can learn to use this marvelous technology available to me as a tool to continue living an active, engaging life.*

I didn't have a lot of time to focus on the difficult parts of my life, because we were celebrating the marvelous milestones occurring in the lives of our family and friends. There were big birthdays with zeros on the end of the number. My older sister was turning 70. Despite the eleven years and the miles that separated us, we are bound by our sisterhood. She had her own difficult path at the time, as her husband had been diagnosed with progressive MS. It would prove to be a difficult journey for him stuck in his degenerating body and for her as the caregiver. She was devoted to him, exhibiting the best of our father and our mother: honorable, creative, innovative, courageous and strong.

Those same traits of my ancestors are carried on in my son, Nathan. He shows strength and endurance and is tender, caring, creative and trustworthy. He was pursuing a master's degree. I always told my children, I don't care if you are a bartender, a trash collector or a doctor, but you must get your college degree first so that you have choices. My daughter carries on the spirit of my parents and their love of houses and projects in her passion for real estate and helping people find the home of their dreams. As parents Oscar and I are proud of all of our children, as they are self-sufficient and kind people. We felt we were reaping the rewards of tending a blended family spread across the many miles. Naturally, there were bumps in the road and things that sometimes got tedious, but I heard whispers calling me to get closer to my son and daughter in Dallas and a new life of growing possibilities.

"God, will you speak up? What shall we do?" I asked. We were celebrating milestones and still travelling, we were also dealing with my increased post-polio symptoms. The wild rushing current of the river of life was very muddy and around this time, we discussed the possibility of Oscar giving up surveying his beloved ships. He was 78 years young and while he was alert and fit for any man, let alone a man of his age, it seemed time to retire, really retire. But with no ships and no RV to occupy his mind, Oscar began to experience mood swings. It was understandable to have an adjustment period. While retirement is what we all work toward, the reality of it can leave a void. My intuition was on high alert. Again, looking below the surface, I asked Oscar to consider seeking assistance with a professional to deal with whatever was going on. He agreed and reached out to the VA. I am always so proud of him and how he is willing to do the hard work of recovery and choosing life even when it's hard. He tells me, "It's our love that gives me a reason to live."

Then another health issue raised its head when Oscar began to have vision problems. He feared for many years that he would end up with the same disease his father had suffered from—and it happened.

"You have macular degeneration." *Dear God, help us.*

"We need to start injections, but first you need emergency retina surgery because you have so much scar tissue, we won't be able to get to the macular for the injections."

We just kept breathing. This was another physical challenge. I am so amazed at how we handle the physical challenges with such calm and grace. The harder challenges are those we face in the darkness of our minds. We rushed Oscar for retina surgery, prepared to face whatever the results might be. It was a miracle. On the follow-up visit after surgery, the retina surgeon was quite pleased with himself for the marvelous job he did. He declared that not only was the retina repaired, but there was now no sign of the macular degeneration. We just kept getting second chances. Accepting the fate of our twisting path, we were met with abounding grace. *You have our attention God. We are listening.*

At this stage of our lives, because of our age and disabilities, we were looking at the future differently. We began to discuss our options. It probably made sense to sell our two-story home sitting on three residential lots. What would that look like? Do we move to another city to be nearer to some of our children? That would seem to make sense at this stage of our lives. What about the roots and friends we had established? *I have a good job. Am I ready to retire? Can I afford to retire?* If I were to quit and move, how would I start over and get a new job at 61 years old? *It will be hard to secure new doctors and build a new community yet again. Mostly, though, am I willing to open my heart to becoming emotionally vulnerable by moving closer to my children?* Living far away, it was more acceptable and understandable if we didn't see much of them. What would happen if we were close by and rejected? I was afraid.

Oscar said that he wanted to return me to Dallas, the city where he had found me. He hoped that by being nearer to my children, when he was gone, I wouldn't be alone. He wanted the children to see me in my everyday life, not just visits.

My daughter said, "Why not?" My son had recently lost his paternal grandfather and told me, "I want the benefit of the next decade with my Pops." *I am not weak, I remind myself. I am strong. I am courageous. I can show up and be seen and be willing to be vulnerable, carrying the hope in my heart for the tender communion we might share.*

I heard again the command to "Fear Not," and we began to make plans to move 200 miles north to the Dallas area, to start over again. Excited and yet fearful, we began to look for homes. Sometimes when life calls, we must take a giant leap of faith and fear not.

Crossing the River

We knew we needed a one-story home with a handicap accessible interior; it would be a wonderful blessing to have a simpler home that would allow us to age in place more comfortably. That narrowed the search quite a bit which was good, because it was daunting how many options there were in the Dallas area. However, we quickly came to see that there was nothing suitable in our price range. Discouragement settled in and I was tempted to call the move off.

Some days I felt courageous, ready to make the difficult journey to cross the wide river that was before me. In our hiking days I crossed a few rivers. Even the narrow trickling rivers were scary because there were always slippery rocks on which I could fall. Using a walking stick to poke around and find the safe next step and watching closely to follow Oscar's lead and how he navigated the rocks, I would successfully get to the other side without falling in. Each time we arrived at a place where we had to cross a river, I was scared and then exhilarated and proud when I stepped on solid ground on the other side.

At this crossing to a new home, I had family on one side coaxing me saying "you can do this" or "you must do this"; and dear friends on the other side warning me, "are you sure you want to do this?" At one point I decided there was too much risk, financially and emotionally, and I changed my mind about moving. Oscar continued to encourage me, reminding me that we needed to open the door to be more available for a daily life with my children. We needed to downsize. I asked, "what about my friends?" I knew the move would be more difficult because it would displace the deep roots I shared with soulful friends. These women had helped me grow up. Their examples, words and friendships were totally real and comfortable. They got me. They carried me through the storms of life and we laughed and celebrated life during the good times. I listened, hoping for clarity.

On a random visit to Dallas, not meant for house-hunting, a single-story townhome came on the market in the suburb I wanted to be in, Plano. We decided to look. I declared out loud, "If this isn't the one, we'll stop looking." It was unoccupied and empty. The moment I walked in the front door I let out a sigh that I'd been holding in for several years. I could see myself in this place. It was an end unit with plantation shutters along the side and back windows, which were open, flooding the home with beautiful sunshine and light. Everything about the place was perfect. There was a study off the entryway with a view of the greenbelt and I could feel it being a perfect sewing room. It had double walk-in closets in the master, and a split floor plan with a long hallway that called for my family gallery. It was a lovely place, but it was also way above our price range.

We took the rest of the evening to consider. Oscar reminded me that he was 80 years old. It wouldn't be much longer before he'd feel too old to move. Listening to him and feeling the longing inside of me for what I wanted, I said "YES. Let's do it." We signed a contract on the place and then went home and put our place on the market. The hardest part was calling my friends to tell them we'd bought a place. Everybody understood, but that did not make it easier. They wished us well and praised us for our courage.

We were very excited about the new place and being nearer to the children, but there were a lot of obstacles to overcome. Besides the physical effort of a move, the emotional upheaval is tremendous. Our emotions were crazy wild like a shaken up soda pop bottle. We were afraid to pop the top for fear everything would spew out. I was sad and happy and scared. Was I ready to face being vulnerable? I was also concerned that the stress of moving might aggravate Oscar's PTSD, which the VA had diagnosed only a few years earlier.

We moved on December 5, 2015 to begin our new life in Plano. The very next week Oscar's nephew called from Michigan to say, "You better get here fast." We knew Oscar's brother was ill, and I had promised to get there as soon as we moved, but he was going downhill fast. We dropped everything and made arrangements to fly out, but he passed away before we could get there. We spent three days with his family—at the funeral home, the lunch afterward and the evening gathering together at the family home, followed the next day by the burial and another lunch. It was a beautiful, loving gathering, but when we got home, we were ready to collapse. We didn't take long to rest, though, because we had a house full of boxes waiting for us.

Meanwhile, one of my dearest friends from Willis, Shirley, was sending me texts saying things like "just drove by your house and burst into tears," or "just drove by your office and burst into tears." I loved her so very much and was grateful to know she missed me as much as I missed her, but I finally asked her to stop sending texts, saying, "Shirley, you're killing me."

Some years earlier I told my dear friend Darlene that when the time came, I would be there to help her and Al. Well, Al had taken a turn for the worse just before we moved. I cried and cried, telling her I was so very sorry I couldn't live up to my promise. Almost every day I would call and talk to her or those surrounding her and Al to check on them and try to be a part of the emotional support team that was walking Al home on his journey to heaven. It was heart-wrenching. My daughter didn't understand when she'd come to the new home and find me crying and beside myself. "You should be happy, Mom. Look at this place and how much closer we are to each other." I was exhausted from the move and the emotional stress Oscar was going through from his younger brother dying, and now my beloved friend was dying too.

Almost immediately, I began to call doctors' offices, trying to find new doctors that would take our insurance. We needed specialists for Oscar and a family doctor. "I'm sorry, we aren't taking new patients," I heard again and again. Beginning to doubt that we had done the right thing, we got the call that our dear friend Al passed away. I only knew one way to get through so much loss and that was one day at a time. We went back to our old neighborhood to visit with our friends about every eight weeks. At our new home, we continued to unpack and settle in.

When the last box was unpacked, Oscar plopped down exhausted, ready to just sit in his easy chair to declare we were done. I looked at him and said, "Oh no, sir, our work has just begun. Now we need to build a life and make social ties to build our new community."

We dove in head first in the deep water. We started visiting churches because we needed that Sunday ritual in our life. The second church we walked into just happened to have their lobby filled with displays of quilts for a Christmas sale. They had a quilting ministry. That got me excited. The people were warm and welcoming and the church sanctuary was beautiful. We never looked further. We found a church home, which would help us put down roots, build relationships and be part of a community.

Then one of my dearest friends from our old neighborhood, sweet Shirley, called to say her cancer was back. *No, this can't be.* She battled cancer twenty years earlier and won. How could it come back after so many years? We quickly drove down for a visit and hugs. Sitting on the couch together holding hands we shared a communion of spirit and soul that was so profound that to this day I tear up thinking about the love I carry in my heart for Shirley. For years we raved to her about the RV trip we made to the Albuquerque balloon festival. We started making plans to all go together the next year, thinking it would help to make forward-looking plans. It would be close quarters, but plans were made for us to snuggle in with Jim and Shirley into their RV for the trip of a lifetime. I especially believe it helps older folks and sick folks to have something planned in the future to give them a reason to push on. *We should not put off until tomorrow what we can do today because we are not guaranteed tomorrow.*

After our move I was living in two worlds, pulled in two directions. On the one hand I had the safety and love of the secure world I'd left behind. On the other hand, I carried hope for the future in our new neighborhood. *How do I know when to hold on and when to let go? I must be able to hold on to all the people I love.*

After Al died, Darlene missed him terribly. Her daughter Jane did the sweetest thing for Darlene's first Mother's Day without Al, writing a letter to her that Jane wanted Darlene to imagine Al had written: "Haven't you noticed the messages I send your way? To tell you to have a better day, we're not apart, I promised you that from the very start. I'm still here with you, just in a different way. I will always be with you each and every day and I hope that you will try to feel me, just in another way."

When Darlene shared this with me, I was so moved and it gave me strength. *I know that God is with me, but what about my loved ones? Blessed be the earth that gave me a connection to the generations I didn't know but can feel them in me. Blessed be the places I travelled that I carry inside of me. Blessed be the ones I love that cannot be physically with me, but I carry also inside of me. In the deepest part of my being, I hear God comforting me. I can apply my gift of hospitality to make room in my heart to carry my loved ones.* I knew this before, but I needed the reminder and reassurance that I hadn't left them behind. They were with me.

Life's disappointments, hardships and losses can make our emotional demons stronger if we let them. The move to Plano would be marked with many hardships. Crossing the wide river was difficult physically but the most slippery rocks were the emotional and spiritual ones. *I cannot let life's difficulties direct me away from my faith. I need to focus and develop new coping skills.* To be honest, it was a constant battle filled with tears that were making the river I was crossing dangerous. I was halfway across the river, frozen in fear, afraid to move, wondering if I should turn back. Some things just take time. Like the seed that takes time to become a tree, it takes time to move through grief and find peace in the day to day of life again. I just had to give this time. I decided I would give it one year before I really knew if I was home. But it is not my way to wait, doing nothing. While the calendar was turning, I was busy building and creating a new life to explore the possibilities that had called me to cross the river. I dug deep to the reservoir of courage and resilience stored in my spirit. In my heart I carried the strength of my parents and my dear friends, all holding my hands and cheering me on. We just had to keep moving forward.

Discipline is part of the fabric of my life. I get up every day with time to be still and consider what I need to do that day. I consider the household chores that need my attention and the budget planning to be done. What will I plan for dinner tonight? What time can I carve out to spend pursuing a passion? This is all part of moving forward, making each day count and being intentional in my life. That's what I do. One slippery rock at a time, I take another step and that's how I get to the other side.

We found a church and finally found doctors. What was next? One evening Oscar asked me if I was going to look for work. We went into debt to make the move, taking on a huge mortgage in our "retirement" years. Finding work would also be a good idea because it was part of planting roots. That night as I went to sleep, I held the idea of work in my heart and asked my subconscious to work on answers in the night. I awoke at 4 a.m. knowing exactly what I needed to do. I was inspired, which to me was another miracle showing up in my life. I went to the computer and Googled real estate law firms within ten miles of my zip code. Six firms popped up. I wrote a cover letter introducing myself and saying I was looking for either permanent part-time work or temporary full time work and explained that I was new to the area and had been at my last job for 13 years. I enclosed my resume and a letter of recommendation. That afternoon I mailed six letters and then I waited. Funny how much waiting life requires. Again, though, I wasn't waiting sitting on a couch. I had my thinking cap on, pondering: how else could I water and grow roots in this new wilderness I was in?

A few years before our move to Plano, our dear friends Lise and Ron gave Oscar his first bridge lessons on a 5-day visit to Canada, as a better alternative to nightly political discussions or watching French television. Then the women's beginner bridge club adopted him as the only man in their club. It's never too late to learn and it was a great skill to bring to a new life. We found that Plano had senior recreation centers. We went and explored. They held weekly open table bridge games. You could just show up and sit down at a table and hope to find a few others to join you. Sure enough, we found folks who played bridge. Then one Sunday morning at church, in line for donuts and coffee, Oscar heard someone from afar and he leaned into me and whispered, "Those women are talking about finding subs for their bridge game. You need to tell them we play." I went over and introduced myself and said my husband and I play bridge. OMG. This was a wonderful open door. We were invited to play as substitutes. The church had couples bridge groups, a women's bridge club and a group playing a new card game we had just learned called Hand and Foot. We made ourselves available for all of it. It is a great way to keep our minds sharp and build friendships.

In my time of quiet contemplation, I considered how I might grow personally in this next phase of my life. I knew my love for cooking and entertaining was a gift for hospitality. That gift would help me open our home to build new relationships and strengthen some of the old ones. My passion for digging in the dirt would be limited in this new place because the homeowners' association only allowed potted plants. While I could add my own touches and get my hands in the dirt with container gardening, it would not take as much time as it used to. Still waiting to hear if any jobs would come my way, I was nesting and settling in and listening. I took some time to set up my sewing room, hanging my appliqué quilt of Mary cradling Jesus in a quilt she would have made if she were a quilter. Mary would call to me, inviting me into the space of the sewing room. It was as if her gentle voice came rolling across mountains, calling me to come closer.

In the last few years, I attended a few quilting retreats at my sister's home in Idaho. The quilting and fellowship seemed quite holy to me. I wanted to learn more. Another miracle happened. Some people might say I just had a brainstorm, but I believe that when I have inspired thoughts or see a path with clarity in my heart, that is another miracle. I woke one day and realized I needed to find a local quilt guild. No one ever mentioned that to me, but I just knew that was the answer. Again—technology blessed me because I was able to Google and find a guild. They were looking to form new sewing bees and I responded saying I wanted to join. I was quilting with the church for World Relief quilts and I had a few basic quilting skills that I was using to make quilts for family and friends. I was hungry—no, starving—to learn more.

I immersed myself into the world of quilts, wanting to learn about styles and techniques and thread and all the various media used to create works of art through textiles. I wanted to challenge myself. My intuition served me well, knowing this new creative calling would help me find the correct balance of tension in my new home. Quilters talk about having a proper thread tension for quilting and define that as when the bottom and top threads meet in the middle with just the right tension and are, therefore, balanced. I stepped into a world where exploring my passion was enriching my days and giving me strength, joy, energy and balance. Creativity is a solution to conflict. My mind began to fill with color and texture and thread. Everything I saw I began to think, "That would make a wonderful quilt." *Praise God from whom all blessings flow. God, thank you for bringing this wonderful passion into my life. This blessing helps me fill my mind with joy. Please direct my path as I discover what will bring me peace and challenge me and help me in my everyday life.*

Life was so busy that I didn't even realize that I was waiting to hear a response to the letters and resume I sent out. Three months to the day before my 62nd birthday, when I qualified to apply for early Social Security, the phone rang. They didn't have any openings in their law firm, but my resume fit and they wanted to meet. OMG. I met with one of the partners, who was very personable. The offices were quite nice. It was the first interview I'd ever been on where the boss gave me a pop quiz asking me to define terminology. We talked about what "part-time" meant to me. He asked about my life. I know that a good employer wants to hire more than knowledgeable people, they want well-rounded individuals. He said they could perhaps make a place for me if I'd be happy with only 2 days a week. When I said that would be perfect, he said he'd talk to his partner and get back with me.

The next day he called to offer me a position at the firm. Overwhelmed with gratitude for the doors that just kept opening, I was reminded again of the saying I held in my heart and quoted many times in my life: "To the person who has achieved inner clarity, new paths appear and doors open without the need to knock." Maybe I had knocked on a few doors, but it was the inner clarity that helped me recognize that I should walk through these doors with gratitude and appreciation.

My life was filling up. I settled into my new job and we began to build a social network in this new home of ours. My quilting was exploding. I wasn't afraid to try anything. I made a marvelous pieced throw-size quilt with dachshunds for my daughter. I made a queen-size quilt using strips creating a heart in the center as a wedding gift for a granddaughter. I explored adding embellishments to quilts and realized that I was uncovering an artistry inside of me that I didn't know lived there. There were retreats and workshops and so much to learn. *I am so very grateful for this world of quilting helping me learn to be creative and introducing me to a wonderful circle of women. I am grateful that my parents taught me to play bridge and that all these years later the fellowship and card playing helps me build and maintain community. I am so grateful to find another church home where I can exercise my faith.*

We crossed the river and were building a new life, developing and putting into place new strategies for our future. I knew we did the right thing in getting to a place more suitable for aging in place. We continued to do some traveling. We met friends in Canada to check off a bucket list item and see Niagara Falls on the Canadian side, which was exhilarating. We took a car trip to Georgia for a granddaughter's wedding and on the way, we circled north to make a sojourn to my old commune property.

It was the third time I'd been back to the property. I walked the grounds and went and sat by the river that ran behind the old church sanctuary and hotel lodging where I once lived. It seemed peaceful now. There had been a time when I had been afraid to cross that river. There was only a forest on the other side but to me it represented the world I feared. *God, here I am. I have no words. Please hear the groaning in my heart. Thank you for helping me to grow in your love and to live my faith now in freedom, not in fear.* When we got in the car and drove away, I knew I could let it go. Sure, I still have the memories and the reels of shame and fear that get turned on in my head with voices I don't want to hear, but that river doesn't scare me anymore because I know I have the ability to cross it safely. I am so very thankful to Oscar and my dear loved ones for walking that road with me and holding my hand and supporting me through that journey.

After a joyous wedding celebration with the family, we made our way back home. I went in the sewing room and ran my hand over the fabrics on the table. We nestled in and picked up our comfortable daily routine. We were home now, thankful and peaceful. The holidays were just around the corner, and I did not yet know that this holiday season would begin a very difficult year of loss and grief. My dear, sweet friend Shirley lost her battle with cancer. She was gone.

I cried a river that month. We went to visit with her husband after the funeral and he asked me if I'd have time to help him clean out her craft room. Darlene and Valerie and I went over to help Jim clean out the room.

"Take whatever you want," he said, "and we'll donate the rest."

Shirley dabbled in every kind of craft. She had flower arranging supplies, needle work stuff, and oodles of yarn for crochet work. We sorted everything with heavy hearts. I found a little canvas bag that Shirley always toted with her on RV trips. I took it to use for my travel; I could put a book in it or some handiwork and feel her presence with me. When we came to the quilting section, I took a deep breath. There was one bag that had finished blocks in it. I remembered a few years back Shirley asked me to help her with a project. She had the squares arranged on a bed and wanted advice on how to assemble them together into a quilt. At the time

I had no idea, because I was not yet a quilter. Being a quilter now, I spoke up and said that I'd like to take the squares. Then there was another bag with twelve envelopes from 1998 that had never been opened. "I'd like to take these also, please," I said.

We finished that day and stood in the room together saying goodbye again to Shirley. We passed lots of hugs around before Oscar and I got on the road and headed home. As I held Shirley in my heart, along with Jim for the journey of grief he was facing, I also held the squares in my hands that Shirley had made and arranged on the bed. I heard a whisper in my heart. *Can you speak up God? What are you asking me to do?* Then I heard the answer, "*Finish Shirley's quilt.*"

I loved every moment of working on that quilt. I assembled the quilt top that Shirley started, putting the squares together, adding sashing and batting and a back. Then I quilted it and returned it to Jim so that his family had Shirley's quilt. It was a gift of love from Shirley and from God to me and then back to Shirley's family again. The project blessed me with quiet introspective time. I knew my quilting was a calling and a gift. Shirley's quilt was more than a project. It gave me hope. I was able to weave together the past while healing the present and infusing my heart with hope for the future.

Finishing Shirley's quilt was pure inspiration. It wasn't my own design, but it gave me confidence and purpose. It was around this time that I decided to upgrade my sewing machine. I bought a table-top machine with a 12" wide throat so that I could do the actual quilting with more space. I loved my machine so much and found so much enjoyment and peace spending time with her that I decided she needed a name. I named her Grace because I feel grace when I spend time with this creative passion that has filled my life. Every free moment I just want to quilt.

Everything I saw became a possible subject for a quilt. Scrolling through Facebook one day, I saw a picture of women with outstretched arms holding hands and dancing. It had a quote underneath about the circle of women around us. I printed the picture out and put it on the wall in my sewing room and looked at it for a long time. It reminded me every day how much the women in my life mean to me. We sing, we cry, we dance and with empathy and love we encourage each other along the way. I was still a new quilter and knew nothing about making my own pattern, but I knew this picture needed to be a quilt. I wanted to hang it in my new office so that my circle of friends would be with me every day. Inspiration happens fast. It floods my being and with clarity I knew I had to follow this idea—not someday or somehow, but *now*. I took the picture to a local quilt shop and started picking colors for the women's dresses. The women don't have details in their faces, because over years the women evolve. They each have different hair and skin colors. The way they are outstretched to each other shows dancing, movement and strength.

As I was cutting pieces and thinking of ideas and planning how to do the quilt, I was cheered on by my new circle of women in the quilting bee I had joined. *Thank you, God, for this marvelous blessing.* I decided to add a technique to the quilt, teaching myself through YouTube videos how to trapunto the dresses to give them a puffy three-dimensional texture. I cannot begin to describe how much this quilted circle of women meant to me. I loved everything the art quilt depicted, and the confidence and joy it brought to my life. It redefined life for me, making me realize that I didn't just have another hobby. When people ask "what do you do?" they usually mean, what work do you do for a living, but now when I am asked that question, my answer is, hands down—I am a quilter!

My Circle quilt hung in my office for a while before my new friends encouraged me to show it at the Plano Quilt Festival. They said it was a juried show and therefore it would be helpful for me as a new quilter, because I would receive feedback from the judges. This sounded intimidating to me, but I learned long ago to face my fears, not run from them. I entered "My Circle," not expecting anything other than the joy of sharing my inspiration. When the piece received an honorable mention, I was so thrilled to receive that affirmation. It helped me to trust my intuition in an entirely different way. My journey into the world of quilting began with a dream to make utility quilts for people in need. I'd come a long way in a short time and I was so grateful that I listened to the calling of my heart. Among the fabrics and the threads and the patterns and the imagination I find peace and purpose.

During the following year, my sister's husband began to decline rapidly. MS is a horrible disease. My brothers and I flew to Idaho to be with my sister to give her our support and love and to offer encouragement for the difficult role of caregiver that she had assumed. We talked about how difficult the aging process is. The four us could discuss most anything and we talked about long-term care and how lucky we were that our parents taught by example how to walk this part of our earthly journey. The subject of aging and long-term care and end of life wishes is just part of real life and sometimes a topic of discussion with friends over dinner or cocktails. It is a gift we give our family to make arrangements and/or make our wishes clear. I feel blessed to have grown up in a family that doesn't shy away from the discussion and to have friends that share their ideas and experiences so that I can incorporate their wisdom into my planning. We never know for sure how life will unfold, but most of my friends and family have legal documents such as wills, medical and business powers of attorney. Some even have prepaid funeral arrangements. Shortly after Oscar and I moved, we went ahead and followed my mother's example and purchased a cremation plan through Neptune Society so that our children wouldn't have to make those arrangements. A few of our children think it's morbid to discuss, but working for attorneys my entire career and being married to someone eighteen years older than myself has taught me that it is kinder to myself and those around me to have some plans made ahead of time. One day at this new church of ours I asked the music director, whom I didn't know very well, if he thought he could play Willie Nelson's song, "On the Road Again," on the organ for a funeral. He assured me he could do a version. We laughed and I said, OK, I guess we can plan to have our funeral in this church then.

Oscar was continuing with his treatment for the PTSD that had been diagnosed a few years earlier. He was in the process of developing coping skills for it and I was learning how to help him. He had a few physical challenges, mostly associated with difficulties he was having with swallowing. One of our favorite winter dishes is my all-day crockpot beef stew. One day a piece of the soft tender meat got stuck in Oscar's throat. I didn't know he had struggled all night long with that piece lodged half way down his esophagus. The next morning, we made a visit to the ER and he had an emergency endoscopy to clear his passage. He was already following a GERD diet prescribed years earlier when he was diagnosed with Barrett's esophagus, which is a precancerous cell found in the esophagus, often caused by unknown, untreated or undiagnosed acid reflux. Now the gastro doctor suggested there might be more going on and we should see a specialist. There was always something.

Life is like one of the quilts that I admire from a distance and then, when I get up closer and examine the detail of its pieces and layers, it becomes even more spectacular and amazing because I recognize and appreciate the hard work, inspiration and execution of the techniques needed to weave a work of art. My life was imitating a quilt, with many layers and lots of hard work. Oscar and I were both dealing with physical and emotional challenges. My bionic DBS brace was irritating my skin. Conflicting recommendations left me wondering what direction to take. Oscar suggested I try not wearing it for a bit, to give my skin a rest, relying more on my old friend, the cane.

In the meantime, I visited with a new neurologist because I was experiencing numbness in one arm. I was afraid the post-polio was affecting my previously paralyzed arm. The doctor said she did not believe it was related. She sent me for physical therapy for my arm, and asked the staff to work on my balance issue and my drop foot while I was there. She didn't believe there was nothing that could be done. Here in the middle of grief for loved ones and worry for my husband, I found hope in this one small doctor's office in the middle of my new hometown. Somehow, I just knew that I was about to have another miracle show up in my life.

Sure enough, with physical therapy I was able to lift my right big toe off the floor. My foot is still deformed, crooked and dropped. But the professional opinion was now that I should no longer use the brace on my foot and leg. In fact, bracing could cause further atrophy and, therefore was not recommended. *OMG. I am free to walk again without a brace. Marvelous miracles woven in the fabric of my life give me joy and hope. Now I hope to be able to have more energy to deal with the other challenges that I face in my life.*

Just around the corner we were facing a raging rapid part of the river. We always spent New Year's Eve with friends. Sometimes we'd gather with a group and go to someplace for dinner and dancing joining the festivities of celebrating with hats and horns. The last few years, we'd go for dinner and back to someone's home for an evening of bridge, with laughter and stories. This time we drove the 200 miles south to stay with our friends to enjoy a weekend of reminiscing and playing cards and dreaming of our next adventure. We made it until midnight and off to bed we went.

In the middle of night, the phone rang, which is never good. Oscar's son Gerard was in the hospital. "Hurry!" Oscar's daughter cried.

We scheduled a flight for the next afternoon and raced the 200 miles up I-45 to quickly pack and rush to the airport for our flight. It had been eighteen years since we had seen Gerard. All those years Gerard never owned his own home and he rarely worked. He lived part of the year with Oscar's sister and part of the year with his mother. If we were going to be in a city where he was, we always hoped to see him, but he always made sure to be gone. We never lost hope and we always prayed.

A daughter picked us up in Atlanta and took us to the hospital. That first evening was an amazing circle of love. Everyone was so glad Oscar had made it in time. Even his first wife hugged me and thanked me for getting Oscar there. We all thought the next day they would remove Gerard's tubes and let him go to heaven.

On the way to the hospital the next day, I received a shocking phone call. One of my best friends, Don Allen, the man I had trusted enough to walk me down the aisle and give me away to Oscar, had passed away from a heart attack. I burst into sobbing tears sitting in the car with my stepdaughter and Oscar. We were getting ready to go into the hospital to say goodbye to Gerard. Heavy with grief we all held hands and held each other up, infusing ourselves with strength and love as we walked toward intensive care.

When we gathered, everything had changed. The doctors and nurses were saying that perhaps Gerard was not at the end of his life. It was hard to separate all the things he was suffering from. He had been an alcoholic for twenty years and he was going through withdrawals. He smoked more than a pack of cigarettes a day for forty years and was suffering from COPD, a chronic lung disease. These two diseases, combined with malnutrition from years of poor eating habits, left him weak, sick and fighting for his life.

A nurse asked to speak to just Oscar and myself. She said the family was emotional and maybe not really hearing what was being said. She didn't want to remove Gerard's tubes. She was hoping to have a few more days to try to get him to rally.

We gathered the family and passed on the conversation. It was in direct conflict with what they had been hearing for the few days before we arrived. The family was confused and some were angry, partly because Gerard didn't have any legal documents designating his wishes and according to state law, since he had no wife, the decisions fell to a parent. Not knowing that law, one daughter told the hospital that Gerard's mother was "mentally unable" to make those decisions. She did not say it out of ill intention; she, like everyone else, knew that Gerard wanted his sister to watch out for him. It didn't matter, however; the hospital said, with no legal papers, the decisions legally fell to a parent. Since they had been told the mother was unable, they looked to Oscar, the estranged father. Life and love got messy again, in ways that were heart-wrenching for everyone.

Gerard continued to linger and we decided we should say our goodbyes and head home. We didn't think he'd recover, despite the new hope the nurses were giving. Oscar had his time with Gerard to tell him we never stopped loving him. The hospital authorities told us that if Oscar wasn't there, other family members could give direction. We hoped that would keep the peace. Only a few days after we returned home Gerard passed away at the age of 59, from complications due to chronic lung disease.

We all survive a lot of loss in our lives, but the grief of losing a child is horrific. We actually lost Gerard many years earlier, but that earlier loss had a lining of hope in it. Feeling hopeless and so despondent, we went home to walk the long journey of grief. Not only had I lost another dear friend, but Oscar lost his son. We were in shock. Then, just a few weeks later, the phone rang and it was my sister calling to tell me her husband had passed. In less than three weeks we lost three loved ones.

We were prepared for this time of desert wilderness and grief. We had rich strategies in place that we developed and incorporated into our lives to help us on this journey. We reached out and sought the help we needed. I insisted Oscar see a professional for grief counseling. I was so proud of him that he was willing again to seek help from his VA psychiatrist. The loss of a child, compounded by the fact that Gerard had been estranged from him; this, coupled with the fallout from the rest of the family drama, was unsettling to say the least. We prayed for rest for our weary souls. Our minds wrestled with the demons of the "what if's." We needed to find balance in allowing time to remember and reminisce without lingering too long. We found peace in the daily chores and habits of our life. The simple daily ritual of making a bed, taking a shower and walking the dog helped us face each new day. We had to keep moving. Our church community helped, reaching out to Oscar to offer support during his grief. Daily rituals, work, therapy, community and faith in action came to our rescue.

I had my own grief and regrets regarding the losses and deaths, but it was very clear to me how I would survive this wilderness journey of grief: I would call on the well of faith in my heart and I would find help from the world of quilting, the creative passion that stirred in my being, continuing to give me inspiration, solace and purpose. There were two massive quilting projects that called to me. I had a pattern for three angels designed to be about 12" x 20." I wanted to blow them up to about 48" x 54," each to be hung side by side in the sanctuary of our church. This was the right time to spend with those angels. They engulfed every corner of my heart and mind. At the end of a day, I would talk to them and say goodnight. In the morning I could hear them singing, calling me into their beauty. I was so excited to see the pieces come together.

I would ask Oscar, "Do you hear that?"

"What?"

"The angels are singing."

The two of us would stand tenderly holding hands and beholding the angels with us. It was a loving journey that carried us both. When the angels named Love, Hope and Faith were done I dedicated them to our church, reminding everyone that there are angels indeed that live among us. We should stay alert and listen and watch, keeping our hearts open. During the making of the angels my creative passion grew in leaps and bounds.

Then I remembered the unopened envelopes from Shirley's craft room. I got them out and opened them up to investigate what they contained. There were twelve envelopes, each containing fabric and directions for one quilt block. OMG. This was from a Block of the Month club Shirley had joined in 1998 and never even opened the envelopes. While the Angels were singing, I heard God and Shirley calling to me, inviting me to come in closer. It was perfect timing. A Block of the Month is meant to start in January to take you through the year. I was only one month behind so it wasn't hard to catch up. Every month that year, I spent a day with Shirley putting together a block. At the end of the year, I had a quilt top and when I got it sandwiched with batting and a back put on it, I quilted it. *God, thank you for encouraging me to pursue this creative passion and for the purpose and peace that it brings me. Thank you that Oscar shows so much pleasure in seeing me pursue this passion. Thank you for inspiring me.* I knew I would keep this quilt close to me forever. This quilt is warmth and love from God and Shirley. It is warmth and love from Oscar because of his tender encouragement. It is warmth and love because of my friends and family, who cheer me on in my progress and passion. The journey of artistic growth fuels me with confidence, lifting my spirits. Quilting is one of the best tools I have in my survival toolbox.

I let myself pray for a special miracle for Oscar now. Besides his walk through grief, he was facing physical challenges. He had been diagnosed with Achalasia, a rare disease of the esophagus. It was a natural time of life to worry about the challenges of aging.

Please God help Oscar to see in himself the man I see. Restore in him comfort and peace.

The answer came in another phone call, from Oscar's old friend and shipmate, USCG Ret. Admiral Thad Allen. Thad was being honored for his many contributions to the men and women of the Coast Guard, and the U.S. Coast Guard Foundation was naming a scholarship after him. He asked if we could travel to Houston to be there with him for the fundraiser.

With pride, Oscar watched Thad Allen rise through the ranks as a leader. He was always gracious to invite Oscar to attend his change of commands as his career advanced. Thad's resume is long and his service to our country is great. He became an admiral and the Commandant. Even after retirement, he serves our country with his knowledge and ability to connect people and inspire them to use their gifts for the greater good of our country. It was unbelievable timing for Oscar to receive this invitation. *Thank you, God, for providing a miracle through Thad.*

There was a cocktail party before the dinner, and folks kept coming up to Oscar. They would see his name tag and comment, saying how many good things they had heard about him. It was strange because Oscar didn't even know these people. It was time to go into dinner. Wowzer. The ballroom was set up for sit-down dinner for well over 500 people. At our table of eight Oscar was seated next to the then-current Vice Commandant of the Coast Guard. We said our introductions around the table and heard more comments like, "Oh—you're Oscar Poppe."

Then the presentation began. It was time to see a film highlighting Thad Allen's amazing career and work. After the film and testimonies from some of the people he had touched, Thad got up to talk. It was a time to shine a light on Thad, but it only took a few minutes for him to graciously turn the light away from himself and shine it on Oscar. He told the story of this one time, on this one day, when one split moment changed the life of many men. It also changed my life because it colored the background of our life together. Only one year earlier, Thad asked Oscar to write his version of that day. In Oscar's own words, here is the story of that day:

A Day on the Andy

During the months of September and October 1971, the USCGC Androscoggin was in the USCG Shipyard, Baltimore, MD undergoing scheduled maintenance after returning from a tour of duty in Vietnam. We were at the end of the shipyard period.

On October 19th, the Andy was moored with shore power and with sanitation and water being supplied from shore. The vessel was almost done with repairs and we were almost ready to leave the shipyard. Captain McDonough and I were at the shipyard maintenance office, which was located at the head of the pier. We could see the Andy from the office windows. We were just finishing up with the meeting, when I looked out the window and saw smoke coming from the Andy. I hollered to the captain, "the ships on fire!" I saw smoke from the ship and it had to be a fire.

The captain and I left the office and ran to the ship. We arrived at the ship and boarded at the forward gangway. It appeared the ship had been abandoned and most of the crew was on the pier. The OOD (Officer on Deck) met us as we came on board and said there was a fire in the forward crew berthing. He confirmed that the crew was on the pier because they were having a crew muster. He also said that some of the crew appeared to be missing. The ship was without power and water making it a dead ship, which added to the confusion.

I told the OOD to complete the muster and have all of my engineers return to the ship. I directed the water pressure restored and the men to follow me. The OOD looked at the captain for orders. Captain McDonough told him to do as Lieutenant Poppe directed. At this time, we were advised that approximately 5 to 8 men were unaccounted for and believed to be in the radio room.

By this time my engineers were forming up with me. I divided them into two fire squads to attack the fires in the berthing area on port and starboard side. It was confirmed now that some men were trapped in the radio room.

I then started to form a separate party to go after the men trapped in the radio room. We did not know who was trapped or how many. I called for some OBA's (oxygen breathing apparatus). I gave one OBA to the petty officer damage control man and another to Chief Warrant Officer (CWO) Walters. CWO Walters, however, couldn't operate the OBA. We were running out of time so I took the OBA and put it on myself so I could lead the fire party. I told CWO Walters to lead a hose team and keep the water spray on me and the DC as the two of us were going in and up to the radio room. We could not see once inside because of the flames and heavy smoke.

When we arrived at the radio room, I found the door jammed. Somehow, with the help of the Lord, I managed to break the jammed door and push it in.

The first person I saw was Ens. Norm Sealander on his knees. He was at a desk dialing on the ships telephone. I asked, "What the hell are you doing?" He replied, "Calling for help."

I said, "We're here. Let's get out of here."

Ens. Sealander replied that there were more men in the "crypto room." I located Ens. Thad Allen and 4 or 5 other men in the "crypto room" trying to get out through the escape scuttle, which was jammed.

I got everyone together and told them to stay low and hold on to the man in front of them. I shouted, "This is a one-way trip, because I'm not coming back."

We all proceeded to vacate the room and finally made it to the main deck where we commenced to fight the fire in the berthing area. Ens. Thad Allen and Ens. Norm Sealander joined the other hose teams and I was on yet another and we went down into the fire area to finally put that damn fire out. I had no idea how long it was until the fire was out.

Oscar F. Poppe, Jr., LCDR USCG (Ret)

As Thad recognized Oscar for his bravery, a roomful of more than 500 people roared with affection, admiration and applause. It was an amazing event, pouring a renewed energy into Oscar, who is still very humble about his role in the fire. In fact, he didn't tell me about it for many years, and his family only knew about the fire because I told them. He almost received a court-marshal for not following orders on that day. It took a few years, but he was finally awarded a medal for his actions.

Everyone deals with emotions and significant events differently. Oscar didn't deal with how this affected him for almost forty years. When the VA doctor said he had PTSD, we didn't understand. The emotions and events that affected him lay dormant for forty years. "It happens that way for many veterans," the doctor said. Oscar continued to work and be a vital part of the marine industry and felt connected and useful. Then when he decided to retire, really retire, his mind had more time. It wandered to places it had not been in decades.

Again, Oscar led with bravery, facing the demons and nightmares and being willing to seek help and do the hard work necessary to learn how to live with and manage PTSD. In 1985, when I married Oscar, I did so partly because I saw how the men and women who worked for him regarded him, and he them. It didn't matter if it was the captain or a room steward, he was available and helpful equally to all. They loved him, and that spoke volumes to me. After we were married, I learned more and more about this honorable, loyal and faithful man. I'm not saying he was perfect. He had his own scars from the battles of life, starting with being told he couldn't go to college because his kind was destined for the factory. Not believing the naysayers, he forged his own destiny, joining the military. Following in his uncle's footsteps he went to sea. Six years in the Navy and 19 years in the Coast Guard allowed him the opportunity for education. He worked hard despite the negative chants of his family that he couldn't do it, and got enough college to become an officer. He also spent 18 of his 25 years AT SEA!!!

That one time...in 1971 during Oscar's service really defines the man Oscar is at his core. He puts others first. He doesn't think about it. It's just instinct. I don't want that story to be lost. I've spent more than half my life with this man influencing me and encouraging me to go for my dreams. He was my destiny and still is my sun and strength. Do you see how he is a hero to me and very brave for so many reasons? He not only took me on with all my baggage and two more children, but he fought a fire, he fought cancer, he successfully faces PTSD and at 85 years old he is still

Oscar and me at the Marine Corps Ball, 2015

up for an adventure, still learning, still my compass and my light.

Semper Peratus, Always Ready, is the motto of the Coast Guard, which is ingrained in Oscar; this outlook sets the pace for our everyday life. Find strategies. Face our fears. Be prepared. This approach to life suits me perfectly.

Then we found ourselves in a world with COVID. Initially, we put our lives on hold. Then we realized that all of our precisely planned travel needed to be cancelled. We were secluded and closed off from the communities we worked so hard to establish. My office sent me home so I could safely work remotely. We listened for information so that we could be educated, but so much of it was conflicting. We heard anger and discord and screaming in the voices on TV and the Internet, with differences of opinion both over politics and solutions for a pandemic. We decided that this wilderness we found ourselves in again might not be so bad if we spent the time listening to our hearts and resting. We had to focus on the things we could control.

God, thank you for technology and the ability to connect with our communities through zoom meetings. God, thank you for my world of quilting. God, thank you for the love that flows through our blended family. God, thank you that Oscar still has his eyesight and he can spend endless hours reading. God, thank you that we have a comfortable home and food to eat. Help those that are not so lucky. Tell me what I can do to help.

We discovered an app called Trickstercards.com that allowed us see our friends online and play bridge while being in separate cities. What a blessing! We continued to be active while we waited with hopeful anticipation to be safely together again with our loved ones in some form or fashion.

I am very grateful for the coping skills and strategies that are in place in my life. Some of those skills I inherited from my parents, who also enjoyed artistic expression and playing cards. They instilled in me the attitude of overcoming obstacles. Those obstacles don't define who I am, they just make me stronger and determined to find a way around them or over them. I never give up and I just keep on keeping on, because this one time...I was a little girl who learned to walk again after being paralyzed. Cult life didn't stop me. Great loss didn't stop me. I am so grateful for the hospitality that lives in my heart and opened me to find great love and tender moments. I am blessed beyond measure to see the clear water that flows in the river of my life. I get to do the things that bring me peace and joy and love. As I dreamed and listened and followed the whispers in my heart, I found myself forging new paths and exploring all of the endless possibilities. I have found peace through the power of faith, community, purpose and love.

Acknowledgments

.

This book would not have been possible without the many people that have touched me along the way, including:

My daughter Leah, for asking me to write this in the first place and giving me love and encouragement.

My dear son Nathan, for his faithful, wise and considerate heart being always open and loving.

My stepdaughters for the deepest, most real relationships that didn't even have to be and yet they are.

My step-son, who always asks "How are you?" and always says "I love you."

My dear, dear circle of women friends who have crossed my path and walked with me every step of my journey.

My dear brothers and sister for being the most loving, respectful, and fun family I could imagine.

My grandchildren, who have seen me at my worst and at my best and still hug me and love me.

I am blessed beyond measure because I have so many friends and co-workers that have helped me along the way and encouraged me to write this book. My heartfelt love and gratitude to each of you.

Adrienne Poppe works as a real estate paralegal in Plano, Texas. She loves to travel, garden, cook and entertain. Her newest passion, quilting, calls to her most days. Find photos, recipes and ideas at adriennepoppe.com.

Green
Fire
Press

Green Fire Press is an independent publishing company dedicated to supporting authors in producing and distributing high-quality books in fiction or non-fiction, poetry or prose.

Find out more at **Greenfirepress.com**.